WONDERFUL TENNESSEE

Brian Friel was born in Omagh, Co. Tyrone, in 1929. His plays include *Philadelphia, Here I Come!*, *The Loves of Cass McGuire*, *Lovers*, *Freedom of the City*, *Volunteers*, *Living Quarters*, *Faith Healer*, *Translations*, *The Communication Cord* and *Dancing at Lughnasa*.

Michael Etherton, in *Contemporary Irish Dramatists* (Macmillan), writes: 'Brian Friel is one of the most accomplished playwrights working in English today. His work is developed around a central poetic vision which has found, and enhanced, a language of theatre to communicate difficult ideas. This language of drama works through wider poetic sensibilities we actually share with the playwright but which we have lost sight of. Brian Friel sharpens our perceptions and makes us able to understand our human condition and the deepening ironies and contradictions of our age. This is his poetic vision.'

by the same author

THE ENEMY WITHIN

PHILADELPHIA, HERE I COME!

THE LOVES OF CASS MCGUIRE

LOVERS

VOLUNTEERS

LIVING QUARTERS

THE FREEDOM OF THE CITY

THREE SISTERS (translation)

FAITH HEALER

ARISTOCRATS

TRANSLATIONS

THE COMMUNICATION CORD

MAKING HISTORY

FATHERS AND SONS (after Turgenev)

THE LONDON VERTIGO (after Charles Macklin)

DANCING AT LUGHNASA

SELECTED PLAYS OF BRIAN FRIEL
PHILADELPHIA, HERE I COME! THE FREEDOM OF THE CITY,
LIVING QUARTERS, ARISTOCRATS, FAITH HEALER, TRANSLATIONS

WONDERFUL TENNESSEE

Brian Friel

faber and faber
LONDON · BOSTON

First published in 1993
by Faber and Faber Limited
3 Queen Square London WC1N 3AU

Photoset by Parker Typesetting Service, Leicester
Printed in England by Clays Ltd St Ives Plc

A CIP record for this book is available from the
British Library

ISBN 0–571–17123–0

For
D. E. S. MAXWELL

CHARACTERS

Three married couples all in their late thirties/early forties:

TERRY
BERNA

GEORGE
TRISH

FRANK
ANGELA

TERRY is TRISH's brother. ANGELA and BERNA are sisters.

The action takes place on a remote pier in north-west Donegal.
Time: the present.

A stone pier at the end of a headland on the remote coast of
north-west Donegal. The stonework is grained with yellow and
grey lichen. The pier was built in 1905 but has not been used
since the hinterland became depopulated many decades ago.
The pier extends across the full width of the stage. It begins
stage left (the mainland) and juts out into the sea so that it is
surrounded by water on three sides – the auditorium, the area
stage right, and the back wall. (*Left* and *right* from the point of
view of the audience).

From the floor of the pier stone steps lead down to the sea
auditorium. Steps also lead up to the catwalk, eighteen inches
wide and about five feet above the floor of the pier. From the
catwalk one can see over the back wall of the pier (about ten
feet high) and right across the surrounding countryside and
sea.

There are some weather-bleached furnishings lying around
the pier floor: fragments of fishing nets, pieces of lobster pots,
broken fish-boxes. Some rusty bollards and rings. A drift of
sand in the top right-hand corner. Stones once used as weights
inside lobster pots. A listing and rotting wooden stand,
cruciform in shape, on which hangs the remnant of a life-belt.

People can enter and exit only stage left.

Wonderful Tennessee was first performed at the Abbey Theatre, Dublin, on 30 June 1993. The cast was as follows:

TERRY	Donal McCann
BERNA	Ingrid Craigie
GEORGE	Robert Black
TRISH	Marion O'Dwyer
FRANK	John Kavanagh
ANGELA	Catherine Byrne

Director	Patrick Mason
Design	Joe Vanek
Lighting	Mick Hughes

ACT ONE

SCENE ONE

Silence precedes speech.

A very warm day in August. Early afternoon. Silence and complete stillness. Then after a time we become aware that there are natural sounds: the gentle heave of the sea; a passing seagull; the slap and sigh of water against the stone steps. This lasts until we have established both a place and an environment of deep tranquillity and peace.

creation

human sounds

Now we hear another sound from a long distance away – an approaching minibus, and almost as soon as we identify the sound, discrepant and abusive in this idyllic setting, fade in the sound of people singing 'Happy Days are Here Again'. Boisterous singing, raucous singing, slightly tiddley, day-excursion singing that is accompanied on the piano accordion. TRISH sings a solo line and this is greeted with laughter, mockery, cheers, encouragement. Then everybody joins in again.

Now the minibus has arrived and stops at the end of the pier (i.e. stage left off) and the idyllic atmosphere is completely shattered: doors banging; shouting; laughter; a sense of excitement and anticipation; animated, overlapping chatter:

US Stage

TRISH: Help! We're lost!

BERNA: Where are we?

TERRY: This is it.

TRISH: You're lost, Terry; admit it; we're lost.

FRANK: It – is – wonderful!

ANGELA: This can't be it, is it?

TERRY: Believe me – this is it.

I

TRISH: Help!

(FRANK (*off*) *sings the title line of the song*, 'Happy Days are Here Again'.)

ANGELA: Where's this wonderful island? I see no island.

TRISH: We're lost – we're lost – we're lost! Help!

TERRY: This is where we get the boat, Trish.

TRISH: Oh my God – lost!

FRANK: Anybody see my camera?

TRISH: Lost – lost!

TERRY: Isn't it wonderful?

FRANK: Sober up, everybody, please.

ANGELA: You're joking, Terry, aren't you?

TRISH: Lost, I'm telling you. This is the back of nowhere.

TERRY: This is it – believe me.

(GEORGE *plays 'O Mother, I could weep for mirth / Joy fills my heart so fast'.* TRISH *sings,* ' – weep for mirth – ' *and says:*)

TRISH: So could I, George.

(*And* FRANK *simultaneously sings the line,* 'Joy fills my heart so fast' *to* GEORGE'*s accompaniment.*)

BERNA: Mind the step.

ANGELA: Admit it, Terry: you're lost.

BERNA: Here's your camera, Frank.

TRISH: Let me out of here. Help!

FRANK: Thanks, Berna.

TRISH: I'm going straight back with you, Charlie.

ANGELA: What in God's name are we doing here?

TERRY: Admit it – isn't it wonderful?

TRISH: Wonderful, he says! Help!

TERRY: Yes, I think it's wonderful.

FRANK: There's not a house within a hundred miles.

BERNA: Let's all go back with Charlie.

TRISH: Heeeeeeeeelp!

(*Now* GEORGE *begins to play* 'I Want to be Happy'. *Cheers*

2

and mocking laughter at the choice. Through his playing:)

ANGELA: Right, George! So do I!

TRISH: Happy – here?

ANGELA: Yeah–yeah–yeah–yeah! Why not?

BERNA: Happy, happy, happy, happy.

FRANK: Yes, George, yes.

(*And they join in the song and continue talking through it.*)

BERNA: Whose sleeping-bag is this?

TRISH: Mine, Berna. Thank you.

ANGELA: At least we'll get a bit of sun.

TRISH: Hand me that blanket, Berna.

FRANK: We're the first people ever to set foot here.

BERNA: Here's your sun hat, Angela.

FRANK: Careful. I'm closing this door.

TRISH: Help!

(TERRY *enters, animated, laughing, excited. Like all the others he is dressed in colourful summer clothes. He has a sleeping-bag slung over his shoulder and carries two large expensive hampers filled with food and drink.*)

(*As* TERRY *enters, calling, off*) Is this your idea of a joke, Terry?

(GEORGE *stops playing.*)

TERRY: (*On*) What's that?

TRISH: (*Off*) Is this some kind of practical joke?

TERRY: Believe me – it's everything you ever dreamed of.

FRANK: (*Off*) Wonderful!

TERRY: Believe me.

(*And immediately* GEORGE *strikes up 'I Want to be Happy' again.*)

Quite right, George! (*Sings:*) ' . . . But I won't be happy / Till I make you happy, too'.

(GEORGE *continues with the song; and some of the people off join in the singing. But* TERRY'*s laughter suddenly stops. Eagerly, with a hint of anxiety, he searches out the island (at*

3

the back of the auditorium, right) and at the same time in a low, barely audible voice, he mumbles/speaks the words of the song the others are singing off. Now he has found the island. He drops the hampers. He slips the straw hat off his head, holds it against his chest and gazes out to sea. After a few seconds FRANK *enters. Like* TERRY *he is dressed in bright summer clothes.)*

FRANK: The minibus is about to –
    (TERRY *is so intent on the island that he does not hear him.*)
    Terry, your minibus is about to head home and Charlie
    wants to know – (*Calls impatiently:*) Please, Angela!

TERRY: Look, Frank.

FRANK: Turn it down, Angela, would you?

TERRY: There it is.

FRANK: That's a crowd of lunatics you have there. So what
    time tomorrow is Charlie to come back for us?

TERRY: Whenever it's bright.

FRANK: It'll be sort of bright all night, I hope. Let's say –
    what? – seven? – seven thirty?

TERRY: That's fine.

FRANK: Seven thirty OK with you?

TERRY: (*Indifferently*) Fine – fine.
    (*Burst of laughter off.*)

FRANK: Surely to God they can't keep that pace up all night!
    (*As he turns to leave,* BERNA *enters. Dressed for the outing and carrying a hold-all, various bags, a sleeping-bag, etc.*)

BERNA: (*Singing earnestly*) 'When skies are grey and you say
    you are blue –'

FRANK: Certainly am, Berna.
    (*He swings her round in a dance and sings along with her.*)

FRANK and BERNA: 'I'll send the sun smiling through –'

FRANK: Wowo–wow–wow–wow! Hey, Terry; some mover that
    lady of yours! (*Exiting*) Right, Charlie. All settled. Seven
    thirty tomorrow morning.

4

(The moment FRANK *exits* BERNA's *brittle-bright face is transformed with anxiety. She goes quickly to* TERRY's *side and speaks in a low, urgent voice.* GEORGE *suddenly stops playing 'I want to be happy' in mid-phrase and plays 'Jesu, Joy of Man's Desiring'.)*

TRISH: Lovely, George. *(She sings with* GEORGE.*)*

BERNA: I want to go home.

TERRY: There it is, Berna. Look.

BERNA: Take me home, Terry – please.

TERRY: Wonderful, isn't it?

BERNA: Please, Terry.

TERRY: Just for tonight, Berna – just one night. Believe me – you'll love it.

BERNA: Have you any idea how desperately unhappy I am?

TERRY: Berna, I –

BERNA: I don't think I can carry on, Terry.

TERRY: Of course you can carry on. The doctor says you're a
   lot better. *(He reaches out to touch her.)* Did you remember
   to take your pills this morning?
   (The music stops.)

BERNA: *(Quietly, almost with pity)* For God's sake . . .
   *(She moves quickly away from him and busies herself with her
   belongings. The moment she says* 'For God's sake' *the engine
   starts up. Again the overlapping voices off:)*

TRISH: He's going.

ANGELA: See you tomorrow morning.

TRISH: Help!

FRANK: Don't go, Charlie! Don't abandon us!

ANGELA: Thank you, Charlie.

TRISH: Stop him. Don't let him go!
   *(*GEORGE *begins to play 'Aloha' and this is greeted with
   laughter and groans and singing.)*

FRANK: Perfect, George! *(He sings a phrase of the song.)*

TRISH: Come back, Charlie! Help! Come back!

ANGELA: 'Bye, lovely world!

(FRANK *continues singing.*)

TRISH: 'Bye, civilization.

ANGELA: 'Bye, Charlie.

TRISH: Don't forget us, Charlie.

ALL: 'Bye . . . 'bye . . . 'bye . . .

(TERRY *and* BERNA *stand in silence, motionless, watching the departing bus.*)

BERNA: (*Softly*) 'Bye, Charlie . . . 'bye . . .

(*The music, the singing, the shouting all stop. The sound of the departing bus fades away. Silence. Once again the landscape is still and totally silent. Then* ANGELA, *unaccompanied and at half the song's usual tempo, belts out the defiant line –*)

ANGELA: (*Sings*) 'I want to be happy –'

TRISH: Damn right, Angela!

ANGELA: (*Sings*) 'But I won't be happy –'

TRISH: Why not?

ANGELA: (*Sings*) 'Till I make you happy, too.'

(*And at this point she is joined first by* GEORGE *on the accordion, then by* TRISH, *and then, very privately, almost inaudibly, by* BERNA. *After* ANGELA's *first line*, I want to be happy', *slowly accelerate the tempo to normal.*

Now enter – immediately after the line 'Till I make you happy too' – GEORGE, ANGELA, FRANK *and* TRISH (*in that order*); *each holding on to the waist of the person in front; all (except* GEORGE) *singing lustily; all doing a clownish, parodic conga dance, heads rolling, arms flying – a hint of the maenadic. All are dressed in bright summer clothes and each carries some gaudy summer equipment – straw bags, sun hats, sleeping-bags, sun umbrellas, cameras, binoculars, etc., etc. Suddenly the pier becomes a fairground.* GEORGE *is the accordionist. His neck is swathed in a white bandage. On those rare occasions when he speaks his voice is husky and*

6

barely audible. TRISH *has a plastic cup (wine) in one hand.*
ANGELA *swings an empty wine bottle by the neck. The
moment they come on stage* TERRY's *face lights up and
happily, extravagantly, he joins in the singing and the dance.*)

ALL: 'Life's really worth living – '

TRISH: Come on, Berna! Party time!

> (*And after a moment's hesitation* BERNA *joins in the parade
> and the singing with earnest deliberate enthusiasm.*)

ALL: 'When we are mirth-giving –
> Why can't I give some to you?'

> (FRANK *now stands aside and takes a series of rapid
> photographs. Now only* TERRY *and* ANGELA *sing to*
> GEORGE's *accompaniment.*)

TERRY *and* ANGELA: 'When skies are grey – '

TRISH: Terrific, Angela!

TERRY *and* ANGELA: ' – and you say you are blue – '

TERRY: Your wife's a star, Frank.

FRANK: Blessed, amn't I?

ANGELA: (*Solo*) 'I'll send the sun smiling through – '
> Give me your hand, Berna! So –

> (*Now back to the very slow tempo and the exaggerated steps.*
> ANGELA *and* BERNA, *hand in hand, dance/promenade across
> the pier.*)

ANGELA *and* BERNA: 'I want to be happy – '

FRANK: The wonderful sisters!

ANGELA *and* BERNA: 'But I won't be happy
> Till I make you happy too.'

> (ANGELA *suddenly stops and holds her head.*)

ANGELA: Oh God!

> (*The music stops.*)
> The head's beginning to reel!

FRANK: (*Sings*) 'In the good old summer time – '

> (GEORGE *drowns* FRANK's *singing with a very formal 'Amen'
> cadence.*)

7

TERRY: Thank you, George.
　　(*General laughter.* TERRY *holds his hands up.*)
　　And now, my children – please.
TRISH: Quiet, everybody!
TERRY: Your attention, please.
FRANK: Please!
TERRY: I bid you all welcome.
FRANK: Thank you, Terence.
TRISH: Where are we, Terry?
FRANK: Arcadia.
TERRY: Ballybeg pier – where the boat picks us up.
TRISH: County what?
TERRY: County Donegal.
TRISH: God. Bloody Indian territory.
FRANK: Where does the boatman live?
TERRY: Back there. At the end of the sand dunes.
TRISH: (*To* GEORGE) Ballybeg, George. In County Donegal.
　　(GEORGE *nods and smiles.*)
TERRY: Right. So – stage one complete. Welcome again.
ANGELA: Sounds proprietorial, doesn't he?
TERRY: I'm only the sherpa.
TRISH: Only what? (*To* BERNA) What's a sherpa?
FRANK: (*Up on catwalk*) Next parish Boston, folks!
TERRY: (*Privately*) Are you all right?
ANGELA: A little too much wine.
TERRY: And you've changed your hair.
ANGELA: For the big occasion! Of course!
TERRY: Lovely.
　　(*She touches his shoulder quickly, lightly, and moves away.
　　They deposit their belongings at various places along the pier – that
　　place becomes that person's 'territory' for the rest of the night. Now
　　they all move around slowly, silently, assessing the pier itself
　　and its furnishings and the surrounding sea and countryside.*
　　TERRY *watches them. He is anxious to have their approval.*)

(handwritten margin notes: "Gentle Island" / "gaelic" and "SHERPA")

8

Well?

FRANK: (*In approval*) Well–well–well–well.

TERRY: So far so good?

FRANK: So far wonderful, Terry.

TERRY: (*To all*) Isn't it?

FRANK: Wonderful.

(FRANK *comes down from the catwalk.*)

TERRY: Some place, George?

GEORGE: Yes. Yes.

TRISH: Sorry, Terry – where is this again?

FRANK: (*To* TERRY) Permanently lost, that sister of yours.

TERRY: Ballybeg pier.

TRISH: In County – ?

FRANK: Wasting your time, Terry.

TERRY: Donegal. This is where the boat picks us up.

TRISH: You've told me that three times. (*To* GEORGE) The
boat picks us up here.

(GEORGE *nods and smiles. Pause. Again they gaze around,
touching the furnishings, sitting on the bollards. As they move
around* GEORGE *plays 'Jesu, Joy of Man's Desiring'.*
ANGELA *busies herself with her belongings, deliberately
ignoring the surroundings.*)

A long time since this has been used.

TERRY: Not for fifty years.

FRANK: More. I'd say.

TERRY: Well?

FRANK: Listen! Not a sound.

TERRY: Trish?

TRISH: Very . . . remote, isn't it?

TERRY: But worth four hours in that minibus?

TRISH: (*Not quite certain*) Oh yes . . .

FRANK: The bus was fine. It's Charlie's terrible jokes I can't
take. If he were my driver, Terry, I'd muzzle him.

TERRY: (*To* ANGELA) Some place, isn't it?

TRISH: Wonderful, Terry. Isn't it, Berna?

BERNA: Yes.

FRANK: These (*rings*) were made to last.

TERRY: And that stone – all cut by hand. (*Again attempting to include* ANGELA) What do you call that mossy stuff – lichen?

TRISH: And that view! Look!

FRANK: What were these stones for?

TERRY: Weights for lobster pots.

FRANK: Amazing. Another world altogether.

TRISH: Heavenly.

TERRY: Yes.

TRISH: You'd think you could see *beyond* the horizon. It really is wonderful. Oh, my goodness . . . (*To* GEORGE) Ballybeg pier. In County Donegal.

GEORGE: I know, Trish!

TERRY: (*To* ANGELA) What do you think of it?

ANGELA: 'Wonderful' . . . I know another happy song, George. (*She sings the first line of the refrain of 'I Don't Know Why I'm Happy'.* GEORGE *picks it up immediately.*) Yes! He's a genius! (*She sings the second line of the refrain.*)

TERRY: Your wonderful wife – off again.

FRANK: (*Spreading his hands*) Your wonderful sister-in-law. (TERRY *sings the third and fourth line with* ANGELA.)

TERRY: Once more! (*And accompanied by* GEORGE *and with* TRISH *clapping in time they sing the whole refrain again.*) Remember Father singing that every Christmas?

TRISH: Don't remember that. Did he?

ANGELA: Your George is a genius, Trish.

TRISH: I know.

ANGELA: Give me a kiss, George. (*She kisses him.*) You should be wearing a toga and playing a lyre and gorging yourself

10

with black grapes. (*She picks up a wreath of dried seaweed and places it on his head.*) There! Dionysus!

TRISH: I have a suggestion, Terry: let's have the party here.

FRANK: (*Holding up a fragment of the lifebelt*) Anybody drowning?

TERRY: We have a boat coming for us, Trish.

TRISH: We don't have to take it, do we?

TERRY: Yes, we do.

TRISH: Why?

FRANK: Because it's all arranged.

TRISH: Berna, what do you say?

BERNA: I don't care. Here's fine. Here's wonderful.

TRISH: Angela?

ANGELA: I know another happy song!

FRANK: (*Icily*) Angela, we're all trying to –

TERRY: (*Sings*) 'Here we are again – '

ANGELA: That's it!

> (GEORGE *picks up the melody.*)
> (*Sings*) 'Happy as can be – '

TRISH: I know that!

TRISH, TERRY *and* ANGELA: (*Sing together*) 'All good pals and jolly good company.'

> (ANGELA *now continues alone. She hoists up her skirts and does a parodic dance up and down the pier as she sings.*
> TERRY *and* TRISH *clap hands.* ANGELA'*s performance is full and exuberant but at the same time there is a hint of underlying panic.*)

ANGELA: (*Singing and dancing*) 'A kiss for Bernadette,
My darling sister, B.
I think I need a very strong cup of tea.'

FRANK: (*Icily*) Not at all! You're wonderful!

ANGELA: 'I may be slightly drunk
As teachers oughtn't be.
But Frank, my husband,

11

Tra-la-la-la-la-la-lee – '

Oh God . . .

(*She flops on to a bollard.*)

FRANK: Thank you very much. Now – what about this boat,
Terry?

TRISH: I vote we stay here. Berna?

FRANK: Terry's day, Trish.

TRISH: Aren't we all happy enough here?

ANGELA: (*Sings to same air*) 'Today is Terry's day – '

FRANK: (*To* TERRY) What do you say?

TERRY: You think this is great? Believe me, my children, you
ain't seen nuthin' yet.

ANGELA: One final happy song –

FRANK: For Christ's sake!

ANGELA: And despite my husband's encouragement the last
happy song I'll sing.

TRISH: Yes, Angela, sing! Let's have a song!

ANGELA: And this last happy song is for our host, Terry
Martin –

TRISH: My wonderful brother.

FRANK: Mister Terence Martin!

TERRY: Terence Mary Martin.

ANGELA: Concert promoter.

TERRY: She means showman.

ANGELA: Turf accountant.

FRANK: Yeah!

TERRY: She means bookie.

ANGELA: Gambler.

TERRY: She means eejit.

ANGELA: And a man of infinite generosity and kindness.
(*Overlapping voices:*)

GEORGE: Yes!

FRANK: Hear, hear!

ANGELA: Yeah–yeah–yeah!

TRISH: Perfectly true!

FRANK: Yes!

TERRY: (*Embarrassed*) That sho' is me, folks. *(Stove)*

ANGELA: (*Raising a bottle*) To Terence Mary.

TRISH: To Terry and Berna.

ANGELA: Friend, brother-in-law, most generous of –
   (GEORGE *plays another 'Amen' chord that drowns out the rest
   of her speech.*)
   Behave yourself, you!

TERRY: Wait–wait–wait–wait–wait. Give me a hand here, Frank.
   (TERRY *throws open a hamper and produces bottles*.)

FRANK: We're not having the party here, are we?

ANGELA: I want to sing another cheap song.

TERRY: There are more cups in that bag.

ANGELA: You sing, Berna!

BERNA: Later, maybe.

TRISH: It's not champagne, is it?

TERRY: That's what the man sold me.

ANGELA: George! A cheap song!

GEORGE: We'll drink first.

TRISH: Oh God, Terry!

FRANK: Anybody need a cup?

TRISH: A bit mad this, isn't it? What time of day is it? (*To*
   BERNA) Maybe we're all mad, are we?   *Was Hamlet mad?*

BERNA: Maybe.

FRANK: May concerts and gambling and bookmaking always
   prosper.

TRISH: Oh, God, Terry, something wrong with this, isn't there?

TERRY: Why?

ANGELA: (*Sings*) 'Oh, Terry Martin, what can I do?'

TERRY: (*Sings*) 'I took a bus to Ballybeg and I found myself
   with you.' Berna? (*Drink*.)

BERNA: Up to the top, please.

TERRY: (*Softly*) You okay?

13

BERNA: (*Loudly*) That's not the top.

TERRY: Shouldn't you go easy on – ?

BERNA: That's sufficient, thank you.

ANGELA: (*to* FRANK) Both up to the brim, please. (*Cups.*)

FRANK: You'll get your share.

ANGELA: Jesus, how I love a prodigal man! To cheap songs!

TERRY: George? (*Drink.*)

GEORGE: Please.

TRISH: Just a little, Terry.

> (*But* GEORGE *tilts the bottle and fills his cup to overflowing.*)

GEORGE: Lovely. Thanks.

TERRY: Good idea this, isn't it?

TRISH: We're blessed in the weather. He's (GEORGE) looking
> well, isn't he?

TERRY: Great. To the old band, George.

GEORGE: The Dude Ranchers.

TERRY: The Dude Ranchers. The best band ever to tour
> Ireland. How many years were we on the road?

TRISH: Twenty-one.

TERRY: Were we?

GEORGE: A lifetime.

TRISH: A lifetime, he says.

GEORGE: And we'll do it again.

TRISH: You were told not to speak.

TERRY: Yes, we'll do it again! And this time we'll tour the
> world!

> (GEORGE *smiles, spreads his hands and moves away.*)

BERNA: I'll have some more champagne, Frank.

FRANK: On the way.

ANGELA: (*To* BERNA) Shouldn't you go easy on that, love?

FRANK: Don't spare it. Loads more in that hamper.

BERNA: Thank you, Frank.

> (TRISH *and* TERRY *are alone.*)

TERRY: How is he? (*George.*)

14

TRISH: He plays all day long. As if he were afraid to stop. ✗

TERRY: He's looking great.

TRISH: You've got to stop sending that huge cheque every week, Terry.

TERRY: Nothing. It's –

TRISH: We can manage fine.

TERRY: It's only –

TRISH: We don't need it. Honestly.

TERRY: How was the check-up last week?

TRISH: Three months at most.

TERRY: Oh Christ. Does he know?   DEATH

TRISH: He's very brave about it.

TERRY: Is there anything – ?

TRISH: (*Aloud*) Quiet, please! The brother is going to make a speech!

TERRY: The brother is – !

FRANK: Speech! Silence! Speech!

TERRY: The brother is going to do nothing –

FRANK: Glasses all full?
    (*Overlapping talk*:)
    Any more champagne?

TRISH: Listen to the brother.

ANGELA: Good man, Terry.

TRISH: Go ahead.

FRANK: Please! Quiet!

TRISH: And make it short, Terry.

ANGELA: Terence Mary Martin!

FRANK: But first – first – may I say something? To Terry, for whom we all have the utmost respect and affection; and to his lovely Berna; both of whom have made all our lives –

ANGELA: (*Quickly, lightly*) Happy birthday.

FRANK: A very happy –
    (*And the rest is drowned by* GEORGE *playing* '*Happy birthday to you*'. *And everybody joins in the singing.* TERRY *covers his*

15

*face in exaggerated but genuine embarrassment and pretends to
hide behind the lifebelt stand while they sing to him. When the
chorus ends he sings the first two lines of the refrain of 'I'm
Twenty-one Today'. General laughter.*)

TRISH: All right, Terry. One very short speech.

TERRY: No–no–no–no–no. No speeches. May I have your
attention, please? Berna? George?

FRANK: Attention, please.

TERRY: Okay?

(*They all fall silent.* TERRY *points out to sea. They line up
around him –* FRANK, TRISH, BERNA, GEORGE. ANGELA
moves off and stands alone.)

Straight out there. That island. That's where we're going.

FRANK: Yes . . .

TRISH: I'm lost – where? – is it – ?

FRANK: Wonderful . . .

TERRY: (*To* TRISH) Directly in front of you.

FRANK: Further left, Trish.

TERRY: (*To* BERNA) Straight out there.

BERNA: I see it, Terry.

FRANK: (*To* TRISH) Got it?

TRISH: Think so . . .

TERRY: George?

GEORGE: See it.

TERRY: See it, Angela?

(*She does not answer.*)

FRANK: That's no distance out, Terry.

TERRY: I suppose not.

TRISH: It's shaped like a ukulele, is it?

FRANK: That's a perfect circle for God's sake.

TERRY: So. There we are. See it, Angela? Our destination.

ANGELA: (*Softly; toasting*) Our 'destination'.

TRISH: I do see it. Yes.

TERRY: Wonderful, isn't it?

16

BERNA: It's not circular, Frank. That's a rectangle.

TRISH: God, that's miles away, Terry.

TERRY: Is it?

TRISH: Miles. And that's in County Sligo too, is it?

FRANK: Jesus.

TERRY: Donegal.

TRISH: Ah.

TERRY: Wonderful, isn't it?

ANGELA: (*Softly; toasting*) A destination of wonder.

FRANK: (*Coldly*) Aren't you going to join us, Angela?

TRISH: (*To* GEORGE) Not Sligo, George. Still Donegal.

(ANGELA *stands beside the lifebelt stand, leans against it and sings in Marlene Dietrich style the first line of 'Falling in Love Again'.*)

FRANK: Angela, please –

(GEORGE *accompanies her now. She sings the next two lines and breaks off suddenly.* GEORGE *finishes the verse and then stops. Silence again as they all – except* ANGELA *– gaze out at the island, each with his/her thoughts.* ANGELA *takes off her sun hat and hangs it on the arm of the lifebelt stand.*)

TRISH: You never said it was a big island, Terry.

TERRY: It's not big, is it?

¼¼¼¼AE⅜trish; That's a huge island.

TERRY: Is it?

FRANK: Hard to know what size it is – it keeps shimmering.

(*Now for the first time* ANGELA *joins them and looks out to sea.*)

ANGELA: Has it a name, our destination?

TERRY: Oilean Draoichta. What does that mean, all you educated people?

TRISH: That rules me out. Where's our barrister? (BERNA.)

BERNA: Island of Otherness; Island of Mystery.

TRISH: God, it's not spooky, Terry, is it?

BERNA: Not that kind of mystery. The wonderful – the

17

sacred – the mysterious – that kind of mystery.

FRANK: Good girl, Berna!

TRISH: All the same it's beautiful. (*To* GEORGE) Isn't it?

GEORGE: Yes.

TRISH: Dammit, I've lost it again. (*To* TERRY) You're sure it's not a mirage?

(FRANK *catches her head and turns it.*)

FRANK: You're looking away beyond it.

TRISH: Am I?

TERRY: There is a legend that it was once a spectral, floating island that appeared out of the fog every seven years and that fishermen who sighted it saw a beautiful country of hills and valleys, with sheep browsing on the slopes, and cattle in green pastures, and clothes drying on the hedges.

And they say they saw leaves of apple and oak, and heard a bell and the song of coloured birds. Then, as they watched it, the fog devoured it and nothing was seen but the foam swirling on the billow and the tumbling of the dolphins.

TRISH: Will we see dolphins? God, I love dolphins.

ANGELA: You know that by heart.

TERRY: (*Embarrassed*) Do I?

BERNA: When did it stop being spectral?

TERRY: On one of its seven-year appearances fishermen landed on it and lit a fire.

FRANK: What was wrong with that?

TERRY: Fire dispels the enchantment – according to the legend. (*To* ANGELA) You're right. From a pamphlet about the place my father had.

FRANK: Maybe it is a bit like a ukulele.

TERRY: Nearly forgot – shoes off, everybody!

FRANK: What?

TERRY: We're supposed to be barefoot.

FRANK: You're joking, Terry!

18

TRISH: Why barefoot?

TERRY: Don't ask me. That's the custom. That's what people used to do long ago.

(*They slip out of their shoes. And again they gaze out to sea.*)

BERNA: There are bushes on it.

FRANK: Come on, Berna! And clothes drying on the hedges?

BERNA: Whins, I think. Yes; they're whins. And a small hill away to the left.

TRISH: God, you've all powerful eyes.

FRANK: Looks more like clouds to me.

BERNA: A low hill. At the end of that side.

ANGELA: (*To* TERRY) You're our expert. Is there a hill there?

TERRY: Expert! I was there just once with my father. I was only seven at the time.

TRISH: I never heard that story.

TERRY: We fasted from the night before, I remember. And for the night you were on the island you were given only bread and water. (*To* GEORGE) Like some of our digs when we were on the road!

(GEORGE *nods and smiles.* FRANK *now takes a series of photographs – of the others, of the island, of the furnishings of the pier.*)

TRISH: And what did you do out there?

TERRY: I don't remember a lot. There were three beds – you know, mounds of stone – and every time you went round a bed you said certain prayers and then picked up a stone from the bottom of the mound and placed it on the top.

FRANK: Trish! (*Photograph.*)

TRISH: Oh, Frank!

TERRY: And I remember a holy well, and my father filling a bottle with holy water and stuffing the neck with grass – you know, to cork it. And I remember a whin bush beside the well –

TRISH: There! Good for you, Berna!

19

TERRY: And there were crutches and walking sticks hanging on the bush; and bits of cloth – *bratoga*, my father called them – a handkerchief, a piece of a shawl – bleached and turning green from exposure. Votive offerings – isn't that the English word? And there's the ruins of a Middle Age church dedicated to Saint Conall. (*To* FRANK) Isn't that the period you're writing your book about?

FRANK: Something like that. Close enough.

TRISH: But it's not a pilgrimage island now?

TERRY: No, no; that all ended years and years ago.

TRISH: Why?

FRANK: People stopped believing, didn't they?

TERRY: Nobody does that sort of thing nowadays, do they? And when the countryside around here was populated apparently they made poitin out there – that wouldn't have helped the pilgrimage business. There were even stories of drunken orgies.

ANGELA: (*Salute!*) Saint Dionysus.

TRISH: But years ago people went there to be cured?

BERNA: To remember again – to be reminded.

TRISH: To remember what?

FRANK: George! (*Photograph.*)

BERNA: To be in touch again – to attest.

FRANK: Angela! (*Photograph.*)

TERRY: People went there just to make a pilgrimage, Trish.

FRANK: And to see apparitions. Patricia! (*Photograph.*)

TRISH: But you saw crutches on that bush. So people must have been cured there.

FRANK: Apparitions were commonplace in the Middle Ages. Saint Conall must have seen hundreds of apparitions in his day. Terry! (*Photograph.*)

TRISH: Don't be so cheap, Frank.

FRANK: Thousands maybe.

TRISH: (*To* TERRY) Do you believe people were cured there?

20

TERRY: All I know is that at seven years of age just to get sitting up all night was adventure enough for me. The first time I ever saw the dawn. I remember my head was giddy from want of sleep.

TRISH: And Father?

FRANK: Berna! (*Photograph.*)

TRISH: Why did Father go out there? He believed in nothing.

FRANK: You're beautiful.

TRISH: Why did father go out there?

TERRY: For God's sake, Trish! That was another age. To pray – to do penance –

BERNA: To acknowledge – to make acknowledgement.

TERRY: You had another word, Berna – to attest!
(GEORGE *makes a sound.*)
What's that, George?

TRISH: To attest to the mystery, he says.

TERRY: And why not! (*Laughs.*) I'm a bookie for God's sake. All I know is: that's where we'll have our party tonight. OK?

ANGELA: Once when the Greek god Dionysus was going to the island of Naxos he was captured by pirates who took him to be a wealthy prince –

FRANK: You'd never guess. My wife teaches Classics.

ANGELA: But suddenly his chains fell away, and vines and ivy sprouted all over the pirate ship, and the sailors were so frightened they jumped into the sea and turned into dolphins.

TRISH: Will we really see dolphins? God, I love dolphins.
(FRANK *is now up on the catwalk.*)

FRANK: Where does our boat come from?

TERRY: A house just across there. (*To* ANGELA) You know *that* by heart.

FRANK: No house. No boat. Nothing from here to Boston except a derelict church – without a roof.

21

TRISH: I'm sure it's very beautiful out there. But I'd be happy
to settle for this. But if you all . . .
(*Silence as they gaze out again. Then suddenly* ANGELA *leaps
on top of a bollard, flings her hands above her head and
proclaims in the style of an American evangelist:*)
ANGELA: There it is, friends – Oilean Draoichta, our
destination! Wonderful – other – mysterious! Alleluia! So
I ask you to join with me in that most beautiful song,
'Heavenly Sunshine'. Brother George?
(*As* GEORGE *plays a brief introduction:*)
Now – open your minds, your lungs, your arms, your
hearts. All together, brothers and sisters (*Sings*) 'Heavenly
sunshine, heavenly sunshine – '
Can't hear you, friends. 'Flooding my soul with glory
divine – '
(TERRY *now joins her.*)
ANGELA *and* TERRY: 'Heavenly sunshine, heavenly sunshine,
Alleluia, Jesus is mine.'
ANGELA: And one more time! Sister Tricia, Sister Berna – ?
TERRY, TRISH, BERNA *and* ANGELA: (*Sing together*)
'Heavenly sunshine, heavenly sunshine,
Flooding my soul with glory divine,
Heavenly sunshine, heavenly sunshine,
Alleluia, Jesus is mine – '
ANGELA: And one more time, Brother George –
(*But instead of a reprise – and without a break in his playing –
GEORGE goes straight into 'Knees-up, Mother Brown'. This is
greeted with laughter, cheers, derision – voices overlapping:*)
George!
FRANK: Wonderful!
TRISH: Good man, George!
TERRY: Sing it, Angela!
BERNA: I know that one!
(*And they all – except GEORGE – dance around the pier and*

22

sing the chorus at the top of their voices. When they get to the end of the chorus:)

TERRY: One more time!

(*And again they sing the chorus. Just before it ends* FRANK *shouts*:)

FRANK: Quiet, please! Shut up, will you?

(*They fall silent.*)

We have a problem, good brethren. I'm telling you – there is no boat.

ANGELA: Who's for a quick drink?

(TRISH *nods yes.*)

FRANK: And not only is there no boat, there isn't a house within a hundred miles of us.

ANGELA: (*To* TRISH) Champagne?

(TRISH *nods yes.*)

TRISH: (*To* FRANK) Use these. (*Binoculars.*)

TERRY: Yes, there is, Frank. Just beyond the sand dunes.

ANGELA: (*Sings to the air of 'Abide with me'*)

'Beyond the sand dunes

You will find our boat –'

FRANK: Nothing but bogland from here to the mountains. And not a boat from here to the horizon.

TERRY: A thatched cottage – further to your left.

FRANK: Sorry.

TRISH: You're the one with the eyes, Berna.

TERRY: As far as I remember it's down at the very edge of the water.

FRANK: Hold on . . . yes . . . is that not a byre?

TERRY: They're the people who do the ferrying.

FRANK: Deserted, Terry. And there's grass growing out of the thatch.

TERRY: Carlin's the name. Been there for generations.

ANGELA: (*Holding up a bottle*) Berna?

(BERNA *signals no.*)

FRANK: Hold on . . . wait . . . Yes, you're right! There's smoke coming out of the chimney! God, that's a hovel! (*He comes down.*) Right, I'll go and get Carlin. Are we all set to leave?

TERRY: Think so. Aren't we?

FRANK: And he picks us up on the island tomorrow morning – when? – about seven?

TERRY: That's the plan.

FRANK: Right.

ANGELA: (*Sings to the air of 'Abide with me'*)
'That is the place!
That shapes our destiny –'

FRANK: (*As he passes behind* ANGELA, *privately*) You're making a nuisance of yourself.
(ANGELA *sings the title of the song 'I Don't Know Why I'm Happy.'*)
What if Carlin isn't at home?

TRISH: Or refuses to ferry bowsies.

ANGELA: Or is dead.

FRANK: Seriously. What if – ?

TERRY: Someone from the house will take us, Frank. They've been ferrying people for thousands of years.

FRANK: I'm sure they have. All I'm asking is: supposing there is nobody free now to –

TERRY: (*Sharply, impatiently*) Tell him the new owner of the island sent you for him! (*He stops short; tries to laugh.*) I didn't mean to . . . ('*let that out*' *is unsaid.*)
(*Pause.*)

TRISH: Well, aren't you a close one, Terry Martin!

TERRY: I'm sorry. I –

TRISH: You kept that a big secret.

FRANK: You've actually bought Oilean Draoichta?

TERRY: Four months ago. Sight unseen. Ridiculous, isn't it?

ANGELA: So it's your island we're going to?

24

TERRY: Stupid, I know. Heard by accident it was on the market. (*To* ANGELA) Miles from anywhere – good for nothing, isn't it?
(ANGELA *spreads her hands.*)
ANGELA: Challenge for a sherpa.
TERRY: I know it's ridiculous. I know it sounds –
FRANK: This is no mystery tour he's taking us on – he's taking us home! Wonderful, Terry!
TRISH: And I wish you luck with it. Congratulations. (*To* BERNA) So you own your own island, Mrs Martin. Very posh.
BERNA: It's news to me.
TERRY: I was going to tell you all out there tonight – tomorrow morning – whenever. Anyhow . . . (*To* FRANK) Will you get Carlin for us?
FRANK: I'm away. Well done. Terrific!
(FRANK *goes off.* TERRY *feels that some further explanation is necessary.*)
TERRY: Haven't seen it for over forty years . . . and I was always curious to have another look at it . . . obsessed in a kind of way . . . and the fact that it came on the market . . .
TRISH: Good. Great.
(*They drift apart and attend to their belongings.* TERRY *goes to* TRISH.)
All I can say is – you have money to burn.
TERRY: Not true at all, I'm afraid.
TRISH: Berna seems in better form.
TERRY: Do you think so?
TRISH: Plenty of chat out of her in the minibus.
TERRY: She's really most content when she's in the nursing home.
TRISH: (*Very softly*) Mother was right, you know: if you didn't spoil her so much.

25

TERRY: Trish! (*To* GEORGE) Met an old friend of yours in London last week – Michael Robinson.

TRISH: You never did! (*To* GEORGE) He met Michael Robinson in London, George. (*To* TERRY) And how was he?

TERRY: Great . . . fine . . . well, not so good. Bumped into him in a pub. Didn't recognize him – not that I ever knew him well. Actually I thought he was a down-and-out touching me.

TRISH: Michael?

TERRY: I know – awful. Asking very warmly for you (GEORGE). Talked for over an hour about you and him at college together . . . doing your degree . . . and the duets you used to play –

TRISH: Sonatas.

TERRY: That's it – sonatas.

TRISH: Beethoven sonatas.

TERRY: Talked for over an hour. Couldn't shut him up. Eventually I gave him some money and just . . . walked away.

(GEORGE *moves away and sits on a bollard.*)

TRISH: That's all they did for three whole years at college – play piano and violin sonatas – day and night. The Aeolians – that's what they called themselves.

TERRY: He said you talked about going professional.

GEORGE: Maybe . . .

TRISH: They were the stars of the college. Oh such stars they were. Michael was going to be Ireland's first great concert violinist. He could have been, too. And there was absolutely no doubt that George was the new Rakhmaninov – no doubt at all about that. And together they were so brilliant, especially in the Beethoven sonatas. Oh, I can't tell you how brilliant they were . . . Michael Robinson . . . oh my goodness . . .

26

(*Pause.* BERNA *hums the line 'O Mother, I could weep for mirth' and stops suddenly.*)

TERRY: (*To* ANGELA) I know you think it's crass.

ANGELA: What's that?

TERRY: Bookie Buys Island Sight Unseen.

ANGELA: But an island remembered, however vaguely.

TERRY: I did it on impulse. In memory of my father, maybe.

ANGELA: A new venue for rock concerts, wrestling matches?

TERRY: Why not? Bullfights, revivalist meetings. I was afraid you mightn't come this morning.

ANGELA: Terry Martin Productions! Dionysan Nights On Oilean Draoichta!

TERRY: If you hadn't come I'd have called it off.

ANGELA: Celebrate The Passions That Refuse To Be Domesticated!

TERRY: I would have –

ANGELA: Nature Over Culture! Instinct Over Management!

TERRY: Angela –

ANGELA: A Hymn To The Forces That Defy Civilization!

TERRY: Oh God, Angela –

ANGELA: (*Passionately, urgently*) Please, Terry – for Christ's sake – please, not now – not now!

(BERNA *stands on a fish-box and proclaims*:)

BERNA: Lord, it is good for us to be here!

ANGELA: Amen to that, sister!

TERRY: Careful, Berna. That box is rotten.

BERNA: I want to sing a hymn.

ANGELA: Yes! Sing your hymn, Berna!

(BERNA *now sings, her face frozen in a fixed and desperate smile.*)

BERNA: (*Sings*) 'O, Mother, I could weep for mirth –'

TERRY: Berna –

BERNA: 'Joy fills my heart so fast – ' Help me, George!

ANGELA: Help her, George.

27

BERNA: I'll start again. Give me a note.
> (GEORGE *gives her a chord*.)
>
> Thank you.
>> 'O, Mother, I could weep for mirth
>> Joy fills my heart so fast –'
>
> (ANGELA *now sings with her*.)

BERNA *and* ANGELA: 'My soul today is heaven on earth
> O could the transport last.'

TRISH: Good girl, Berna!
> (*Now* TRISH *joins them*.)

BERNA, ANGELA *and* TRISH: 'I think of thee and what thou
>> art –'
>
> (*Now* TERRY *joins them*.)

BERNA, ANGELA, TRISH *and* TERRY: 'Thy majesty, thy state.
> And I keep singing in my heart
> Immaculate! Immaculate!'

SCENE TWO

Before the lights come up we hear GEORGE *playing the entire first verse of 'Oft in the Stilly Night'.*

About twelve hours later – the early hours of the following morning. The pier is lit by a mid summer-night glow that illuminates with an icy, surreal clarity.

The boisterous, day-excursion spirit has long ago evaporated. Waiting for the boat has made them weary and a bit irritable. Each has retreated into his/her own privacy and does not wish to be intruded on.

ANGELA *is sitting on a bollard, gazing without interest through the binoculars in the general direction of the island.* TRISH *is sitting with her back to the pier wall, her arms round her legs, her face on her knees.* FRANK *is on the catwalk and looking towards Carlin's*

28

house. BERNA *is sitting on the edge of the pier (stage right), her legs hanging over the edge of the pier floor.* GEORGE *is sitting on a fish-box, head back, eyes closed, body erect and tense, playing the last bars of the song.* TERRY *looks casually through the hampers, examining the contents, tidying up, killing time.*

The music ends.

TERRY: Anybody for a slice of melting birthday cake?
(*No answer. He continues tidying. Pause.*)
Glass of flat champagne?
(*No answer. He continues tidying. Pause.*)
Venison and apricot compote? Honey gâteau? Ever hear of honey gâteau?

TRISH: Give our heads peace, Terry, would you?

TERRY: Maybe I should bring this cake over to Carlin. Might soften his bark.

FRANK: Hey-hey-hey-hey-hey! Look at that! There's smoke coming from the chimney again!

TRISH: (*Wearily*) Wonderful.

FRANK: He lets the fire die at midnight and then three hours later he lights it up again. What the hell is Mr Carlin up to?

TRISH: We could do with a fire. It's got chilly.

FRANK: What sort of a game is he playing with us?

TERRY: Time has no meaning for a man like that. (*Holds up a small box* .) Cherry and mandarin chartreuse – ? (*To* TRISH) Sorry.
(*Pause.* GEORGE *now plays the full chorus of 'Down by the Cane-brake'. He plays very softly and more slowly than the song is scored. His arrangement with its harmonium-style chords endows the song with the tone and dignity of a hymn. It sounds almost sacred. Immediately after he plays 'Down by the Cane-brake, close by the mill'* ANGELA *looks at him.*)

ANGELA: 'Down by the Cane-brake.'

29

GEORGE: Know it?

ANGELA: Haven't heard it in years.

TERRY: What's a cane-brake?

ANGELA: Shelter-belt of canes, I suppose. Protection against the elements.

TERRY: Ah.

FRANK: If he's not playing some sort of bizarre game with us, then explain why he lights his fire at three in the morning.

ANGELA: He just loves tormenting us.

TRISH: The poor man's cold, Frank.

FRANK: Not that man. That man has no human feelings.

ANGELA: Maybe he wants to dispel the enchantment.

TERRY: Marrons glacés – whatever they are. George?

GEORGE: No, thanks.

FRANK: He has betrayed us, the bastard.

TERRY: He'll come, Frank. Believe me.

TRISH: We could do with a cane-brake here.

FRANK: If he never had any intention of ferrying us across – fine! – say that straight out! 'Sorry, bowsies, no ferrying today.'

TERRY: He'll come.

TRISH: Couldn't we rent his boat from him and row ourselves out?

FRANK: Where's the boat? Has he got a boat?

TERRY: (To TRISH) He'd never allow that.

TRISH: Why not?

TERRY: That's his job.

TRISH: Too late to go out now anyway.

TERRY: It's only ten to three. We'll still make it – believe me.

TRISH: Of course, when I proposed we spend the night here, I was shouted down. Perverse – that's what you are.

FRANK: 'Give me a while at the turf, sir. That's all I need.' And four hours later, 'A mouthful of tea and I'll be over behind you.'

30

TRISH: Maybe he's past ferrying people. Is he very old?

FRANK: Ancient; and filthy; and toothless. And bloody smiling all the time.

ANGELA: Forget Mr Carlin, my darlings. Put Mr Carlin out of your thoughts.

FRANK: God, I always hated peasants.

TRISH: And bloody Sligo peasants are the worst, I'm sure.

TERRY: He'll come. Believe me. He'll come.

ANGELA: 'Believe me – believe me' – I suppose it's enviable in a way. Is it?

TERRY: What is?

(ANGELA *does not answer. She goes to* BERNA *at the end of the pier*.)

ANGELA: What's the water like?

BERNA: Warm. Warmish.

ANGELA: Wouldn't mind a swim. Brighten us all up. (*She hugs* BERNA *quickly*.) And how's the baby sister? (BERNA *shrugs*.) You're looking much stronger.

BERNA: Am I?

ANGELA: Terry says you'll be back in the practice in a month.

BERNA: That's not true. Who's looking after the children tonight?

ANGELA: The McGuires next door.

BERNA: The whole brood?

ANGELA: I know. Hearts of gold.

BERNA: I have a birthday present for young Frankie. I'll drop it in at the weekend.

ANGELA: You have that godson of yours spoiled.

BERNA: No, I'll get Terry to leave it in. The godson has got very . . . tentative with me recently.

ANGELA: You couldn't make that –

BERNA: I make him uneasy. You know how intuitive children are. I think maybe I frighten him.

ANGELA: Frankie's dying about you, Berna.

31

BERNA: Frighten is too strong. When I reach out to touch him he shrinks away from me. I . . . disquiet him. Anyhow. Do you really think I look stronger?

ANGELA: I know you are.

BERNA: Terry thinks the reason for my trouble is that we couldn't have a child. That's what he tells the doctors. And that never worried me all that much. But it's an obsession with him. He's even more neurotic than Trish about not having children. A Martin neurosis, I tell him.

ANGELA: Shhh.

BERNA: And he would have been so good with children. Married the wrong sister, didn't he?

ANGELA: Berna –

BERNA: Oh, yes; oh, yes. When you married Frank a little portion of him atrophied. Then he turned to me. I'm the surrogate.

ANGELA: You've got to –

BERNA: Are you happy, Angela?
(ANGELA *hums 'Happy days are here again'*.)
There are times when I feel I'm . . . about to be happy. That's not bad, is it? Are you laughing at me?

ANGELA: Of course I'm not laughing at you.

BERNA: Maybe that's how most people manage to carry on – 'about to be happy'; the real thing *almost* within grasp, just a step away. Maybe that's the norm. But then there are periods – occasions – when just being alive is . . . unbearable.

TERRY: Marinated quail and quince jelly. God!

TRISH: The delights of the world – you have them all there.

ANGELA: There are times when all of us –

BERNA: He has no happiness with me – Terry. Not even 'about-to-be' happiness. He should leave me. I wouldn't mind if he did. I don't think I'd mind at all. Because in a way I feel I've moved beyond all that. (*She stands up.*) But then what would he do, where would he go?

32

(*She moves away.* ANGELA *picks up the binoculars.*)

TERRY: Six months ago there was a horse called Quince Fruit running at Cheltenham. Worst mistake of my whole life. Practically cleaned me out – Quince Fruit almost ruined me.

(*Pause. Now* BERNA *begins singing the verse of 'Down by the Cane-brake'. Immediately* GEORGE *accompanies her. She sings in the mood* GEORGE *established earlier, softly, quietly, but not quite as slowly as* GEORGE *played the chorus. She tells the story of the song with intimacy and precision, as do the others when they sing or join in, each singing in the same quiet, internal personal way.*)

BERNA: (*Sings*) 'Down by the cane-brake, close by the mill
　　　There lived a blue-eyed girl by the name of Nancy
　　　　　Dill – '

TERRY: (*To* TRISH) Mother's song.
(TRISH *nods.*)

BERNA: (*Sings*) 'I told her that I loved her, I loved her very long,
　　　I'm going to serenade her and this will be my song – '
(TRISH *now sings the chorus with* BERNA.)

BERNA and TRISH: 'Come, my love, come, my boat lies low,
　　　She lies high and dry on the O-hi-o.
　　　Come, my love, come, and come along with me
　　　And I'll take you back to Tennessee.'
(*A very brief bridging passage by* GEORGE. *Then* TERRY *sings alone.*)

TERRY: (*Sings*) 'Down by the cane-brake some happy day
　　　You'll hear a wedding bell a-ringing mighty gay.
　　　I'm going to build a cabin and in a trundle bed
　　　There'll be a blue-eyed baby and all because you said – '
(*Chorus sung by* FRANK, BERNA, TRISH *and* TERRY. *Then* TRISH *alone:*)

TRISH: 'Down by the cane-brake that's where I'll stay

33

Longside of Nancy Dill till we are laid away.
And when we get to heaven and Peter lets us in
I'll start my wings a-flappin' and sing to her again – '
(*Chorus sung by* FRANK, BERNA, TRISH, TERRY *and*
ANGELA. *Then a final cadence from* GEORGE. *Brief pause.*)
What time is it?

TERRY: Just after three.

TRISH: Night, everybody. See you in the morning. 'Bye.
(*Again they all retreat into their privacies.* ANGELA *looks
through the binoculars.*)

TERRY: (*Passing behind* ANGELA) Tennessee still there?

ANGELA: Lost it again.

TERRY: Still there. 'Believe me.'
(*She shrugs and smiles.* TERRY *looks around at them all.
Then he addresses them.*)
I know – I'm sorry – it's a mess. And when we were
planning it, it seemed a wonderful idea. It still is a
wonderful idea. And there's still a good chance we'll make
it – a very good chance. Carlin *will* come. I honestly . . .
Anyhow . . . sorry, sorry . . .
(*Pause.*)

TRISH: (*Sits up.*) I know when I was in Sligo before! Seventeen
years ago – at a bridge congress.

TERRY: Donegal, Trish.

TRISH: No, Sligo. At the old Great Southern Hotel. My
partner was a man –

FRANK: Here he comes! There he is! Look! Look!

TRISH: What? – who? –

FRANK: The boatman! Carlin! With his boat! He's here! He's
bloody here!
(*Suddenly everybody is excited, agitated. They all talk at the
same time:*)

TRISH: Who's here?

TERRY: Carlin.

34

BERNA: Oh God.

TERRY: Where is he?

TRISH: Who's Carlin?

ANGELA: I don't believe it.

TERRY: Great – terrific! Are you sure, Frank?

BERNA: (*Anxious, agitated*) Oh God! – Oh my God! –

ANGELA: The bastard – where is he?

TRISH: Where, Frank? Where?

ANGELA: I don't believe it.

BERNA: Oh, my God!

TERRY: Is he alone? Quiet, please!

BERNA: Oh, my God, Angela –

TERRY: Where is he, Frank?

TRISH: Can you see him?

ANGELA: I don't believe it.

TERRY: Where is he, Frank?

FRANK: 'Wolf!' cried the naughty boy. 'Wolf.'

TRISH: What? Where is he?

FRANK: 'Wolf – wolf.'

BERNA: He's not there at all?

FRANK: 'Fraid not. Woke you up all the same, didn't it?

TERRY: (*Quiet fury*) That is not funny, for Christ's sake.

TRISH: Oh, Frank, how could you?

FRANK: Joke.

ANGELA: (*Calmly*) Damn you, Frank.

FRANK: A joke – that's all.

TERRY: Not funny at all, Frank.

FRANK: Sorry.

TRISH: Oh, Frank, that was cruel.

FRANK: Sorry – sorry – sorry. For God's sake, what's eating
you all?

(*Again they retreat into themselves. And as they do* GEORGE
*plays 'Regina caeli, laetare, alleluia; quia quem meruisti
portare – '. He breaks off mid-phrase. Silence.*)

35

ANGELA: (*Suddenly, with great energy*) All right, everybody! Story time! So we're stuck here! We're going nowhere! We'll pass the night with stories.

TRISH: Good for you, Angela. Yeah–yeah–yeah–yeah!

ANGELA: 'Once upon a time' – who goes first? Terry!

TERRY: I don't know any stories.

TRISH: Yes, you do. He's a wonderful story-teller.

ANGELA: We'll get him later. You start off, Trish.

TRISH: Let someone else start. I'll go second. Berna, tell us one of your law stories.

BERNA: All right. Let me think of one.

TRISH: A clean law story! We'll come back to you. Frank – 'Once upon a time – '

FRANK: Pass.

TERRY: Get it over with, Frank.

TRISH: Come on, Frank. Be a sport. It's only a bit of fun.

FRANK: Later. After Berna.

ANGELA: I think George wants to go first.

FRANK: What about yourself, Terry?

TERRY: Couldn't tell a story to save my life.

ANGELA: Have you a story to tell, George?

TRISH: What's wrong with you all? You go first, Angela. Then a clean law story. Then Frank. Then –

ANGELA: George?

GEORGE: Yes?

TRISH: Then me. Then Terry –

ANGELA: George will go first. Tell us your story, George.

TRISH: Right – I'll kick off.

ANGELA: (*To* GEORGE) 'Once upon a time – '

FRANK: Stop bullying, Angela.

(GEORGE *moves into the centre of the group.*)

TRISH: This woman had ten children, one after the other, and –

ANGELA: Right, George?

36

TERRY: Angela –

ANGELA: (*To* GEORGE) Ready?

TRISH: And the ten children all had red hair like the –

ANGELA: (*To* TRISH) Please. (*To* GEORGE) 'Once upon a
time –'

(*Silence. GEORGE looks at each of them in turn. Then he
plays the first fifteen seconds of the third movement (Presto) of
Beethoven's Sonata No.14 ('Moonlight'). He plays with
astonishing virtuosity, very rapidly, much faster than the piece
is scored, and with an internal fury; so that his performance,
as well as being dazzlingly dextrous and skilful and fast –
because of its dazzling dexterity and skill and speed – seems
close to parody. And then in the middle of a phrase, he
suddenly stops. He bows to them all very formally, as if he had
given a recital in a concert hall.*)

GEORGE: Thank you. Thank you very much.

(*He now removes the accordion and puts it in the case. Pause.*)

TRISH: (*Almost shouting, very emotional, close to tears*) Are you
satisfied now? Happy now, are you? Do you see, you all? –
not one of you is fit to clean his boots!

(*GEORGE now spreads out a sleeping-bag and lies on top of it.
TRISH spreads a rug over him. Pause.*)

BERNA: I'm going for a swim. Anybody coming?

TERRY: Please, Berna; not now.

BERNA: Angela?

TERRY: That water could be dangerous, Berna.

ANGELA: Wait until daybreak. I'll go with you then. I'd love a
swim, too. As soon as it's daylight.

(*FRANK comes down from the catwalk. He goes to* TERRY.)

FRANK: Waiting – just waiting – waiting for anything makes
you a bit edgy, doesn't it? Sorry about that wolf thing.

(*TERRY makes a gesture of dismissal and continues looking
through the hampers.*)

It wasn't meant cruelly. Just stupid.

37

TERRY: Brandied peaches and Romanian truffles. Christ. I order two hampers of good food and they fill them with stuff nobody can eat. (*Holds up a bottle.*) Drop of brandy?

FRANK: If you had some whiskey.

TERRY: Should have.

FRANK: Can't take it neat though.

TERRY: (*Searching hamper*) Of course – everything except water. (*He points to a shallow hollow on the floor of the pier where water has gathered.*) Is that rain water or salt water? (FRANK *dips a finger and tastes it.*)

FRANK: We're in business. (FRANK *scoops some water into a paper cup and makes a drink. Toasts:*) Happy birthday, Terry.

TERRY: That was yesterday.

FRANK: Was it? All the same.

TERRY: How's the book coming on?

FRANK: The finishing post is in sight . . . at last. Time for it, says you, after three-and-a-half years.

TERRY: Great.

FRANK: I know I shouldn't say this but I hope – God damn it, I pray – this is going to be the breakthrough for me. And some instinct tells me it will. Well . . . maybe . . . touch wood.

TERRY: You've told me a dozen times – I'm sorry – clock-making through the ages – is that it?

FRANK: Terence!

TERRY: Sorry.

FRANK: *The Measurement of Time and its Effect on European Civilization.*

TERRY: Ah.

FRANK: I know. But they assure me there is a market for it – not large but worldwide. It *is* fascinating stuff. I never seem to thank you for all your help, Terry.

TERRY: Nothing – nothing. Another splash?

(*He pours more whiskey into the cup.*)

FRANK: How can I thank you adequately? Only for you I'd still
be sitting in that estate agent's office. Instead of which –
ta–ra! – the thrilling life of a journeyman writer,
scrounging commissions. Angela going back to lecturing
after all these years – that was a huge help, too, of course.
And the poor girl hates it, hates it. But your support,
Terry, every bloody week – magnanimous! I hope some
day I'll –

TERRY: Don't talk about it. Please.

FRANK: A new Medici.

TERRY: Is that a horse?

FRANK: You know very well –

TERRY: I'd put money on that myself!

FRANK: Thanks. That's all I can say. Thank you.

(*He finishes his drink rapidly and makes another.* TRISH *puts
a pillow under* GEORGE'*s head.*)

TRISH: Lift your head. Good. Are you warm enough? That's
better.

FRANK: I annoyed Trish a while ago. She said I was cheap,
joking about apparitions out there.

TERRY: She has her hands full.

FRANK: Tough life. Courageous lady.

TERRY: Yes. So – the clock book – when is it going to appear?

FRANK: Another apparition. This time next year, we hope.
Actually I was thinking of doing a chapter on apparitions
– well, visions, hallucinations, whatever.

TERRY: In a book about clocks?

FRANK: Time measurement, Terry! Did you know that the
accurate measurement of time changed monastic practices
in the Middle Ages, when Saint Conall and company
flourished out there? See? You never knew that! Before
that monks prayed a few times during the day – a casual
discipline that depended on nature – maybe at cock-crow,

39

at high noon, when it got too dark to work in the fields.
But Saint Benedict wanted more than that from his
monks: he wanted continuous prayer. And with the
invention of clocks that became possible.

TERRY: But there weren't clocks then, were there?

FRANK: No, no; crude time-pieces; sophisticated egg-timers.
But with these new instruments you could break the
twenty-four hours into exact sections. And once you
could do that, once you could waken your monks up at
fixed hours two or three times a night, suddenly – (*claps
his hands*) – continuous prayer!

TERRY: What has that to do with apparitions?

FRANK: Think about it. At the stroke of midnight – at
2.00 a.m. – at 4.00 a.m. – at 6.00 a.m. – you chase your
monks out of their warm beds. Into a freezing chapel.
Fasting. Deprived of sleep. Repeating the same chant
over and over again. And because they're hungry and
disoriented and giddy for want of sleep and repeating the
same droning chant over and over again, of course they
hallucinate – see apparitions – whatever. Wouldn't you?

TERRY: (*Laughs*) Frank!

FRANK: Honestly! Medieval monks were always seeing
apparitions. Read their books. And all because of the
invention of time-pieces. A word of warning, Terry. Be
careful at matins – that's just before dawn. That's when
you're most susceptible.

TERRY: Is that going to be in your book?!

FRANK: Maybe. Why not? Anything to explain away the
wonderful, the mystery.

TERRY: But you don't believe a word of that, do you?

FRANK: How would I know? But there must be some
explanation, mustn't there? The mystery offends – so the
mystery has to be extracted. (*Points to the island.*) They
had their own way of dealing with it: they embraced it all

40

Donal McCann as Terry.

All photos of the 1993 Broadway cast by Tom Lawlor.

(From left to right) Donal McCann as Terry, Ingrid Craigie as Berna, Marion O'Dwyer (back) as Trish and Catherine Byrne as Angela.

John P. Kavanagh (top) as Frank with Catherine Byrne as Angela.

(From left to right) John P. Kavanagh as Frank, Marion O'Dwyer as Trish, Robert A. Black as George, Ingrid Craigie as Berna and Donal McCann as Terry.

– everything. Yes, yes, yes, they said; why bloody not? A rage for the absolute, Terry – that's what they had. And because their acceptance was so comprehensive, so open, so generous, maybe they *were* put in touch – what do you think? – so intimately in touch that maybe, maybe they actually *did* see.

TERRY: In touch with what? See what?

FRANK: Whatever it is we desire but can't express. What is beyond language. The inexpressible. The ineffable.

TERRY: To spend their lives out there in the Atlantic, I suppose they must have been on to something.

FRANK: And even if they were in touch, even if they actually did see, they couldn't have told us, could they, unless they had the speech of angels? Because there is no vocabulary for the experience. Because language stands baffled before all that and says of what it has attempted to say, 'No, no! That's not it all! No, not at all!' (*He drinks rapidly.*) Or maybe they did write it all down – without benefit of words! That's the only way it could be written, isn't it? A book without words!

TERRY: You've lost me, Frank.

FRANK: And if they accomplished that, they'd have written the last book ever written – and the most wonderful! And then, Terry, then maybe life would cease! (*He laughs. Brief pause.*) Or maybe we've got it all wrong as usual, Terry. Maybe Saint Conall stood on the shores of the island there and gazed across here at Ballybeg and said to his monks, 'Oh, lads, lads, *there* is the end of desire. Whoever lives there lives at the still core of it all. Happy, happy, lucky people.' What do you think? (*FRANK is now very animated. He laughs again. He drinks again.*)

TERRY: That's us – happy people.

FRANK: (*Calls*) Come and join us, Conall! It's all in place here!

41

(*To* TERRY) Well – why not?

TERRY: Indeed.

FRANK: (*Laughs*) Despite appearances.

TERRY: Why not?

(TERRY *fills the outstretched cup again.*)

FRANK: Can't drink it without water.

TERRY: Any left in the holy well?

FRANK: Enough. (*Again he scoops up water and makes a drink.*) Aren't you joining me?

TERRY: Pass this time. To the book.

FRANK: No, no, not to the book. The book's nothing, nothing at all; a silly game of blind man's buff. No, to the other, to the mystery itself, Terry. To the goddamn wonderful, maddening, necessary mystery. (*He shudders as if with cold.*)

TERRY: You're cold in that shirt. Here. Put this on.

(TERRY *takes off his jacket and puts it round* FRANK's *shoulders.*)

That's definitely your colour.

FRANK: And to my goddamn wonderful wife. Is it profane to talk about her in the same breath as the sacred?

TERRY: Is it?

FRANK: Look at her. Now there's an apparition. She's . . . miraculous in that light, isn't she? Fourteen years married and the blood still thunders in my head when I look at her . . . Have you any idea, Terry, have you any idea at all of the turmoil, the panic people like me live in – the journeymen, the clerks of the world? No, no, the goddamn failures for Christ's sake.

TERRY: Frank, you –

FRANK: Of course I am. Husband – father – provider – worthless.

TERRY: Your book will –

FRANK: The great book! (*He makes a huge gesture of dismissal.*)

42

She pretends to believe in it, too. But she's such a bright
woman – she knows, she knows. You both know. Oh,
Jesus, Terry, if only you knew, have you any idea at all
just how fragile it all is . . . ? (*Calls:*) Maybe you should
stay where you are, lads. It's not quite all in place here
yet . . . Damn good whiskey. What is it? Coleraine 1922!
That's very special. May I help myself? (*Proclaims:*)
Lord, it is good for us to be here! Isn't it . . . ?
(*He moves away. Pause.*)

ANGELA: (*Softly, tentatively*) Oh my God . . .
TERRY: What is it?
ANGELA: Oh God, is it . . . ?
TRISH: What's the matter, Angela?
ANGELA: I think – oh God – I think –
TRISH: Angela, are you sick?
ANGELA: There's our boat.
BERNA: Where?
TRISH: Stop that, Angela.
FRANK: Where? Where is it?
    (GEORGE *sits up.*)
BERNA: I see no boat.
TERRY: Where is it, Angela?
FRANK: Are you sure?
TRISH: Where? – show me – where? (*To* GEORGE) The boat's
    here, she says.
ANGELA: (*Points*) There. It is, Terry, isn't it?
TRISH: Is it, Terry?
BERNA: There is no boat.
ANGELA: Oh God, Terry, that's our boat – isn't it?
TRISH: Point to it.
ANGELA: Maybe it's only – can you see nothing? – that patch
    of light on the water – just beyond that I thought I saw –
FRANK: Nothing. There's nothing.
TRISH: Where's the patch of light?

43

BERNA: There's no patch of light.

TERRY: Is it anywhere near that mist?

FRANK: Nothing. All in her head.

ANGELA: He's right . . . sorry . . . nothing . . . for a minute I
was certain . . . sorry . . .

BERNA: You shouldn't do that, Angela.

ANGELA: Sorry.

BERNA: You really shouldn't do that.

ANGELA: I'm very sorry. I really am.

TERRY: There *is* a patch of light there; and if you stare at it
long enough it seems to make shapes . . . Anyhow, no
harm done.

(*Pause.*)

(*Privately to* ANGELA) I ordered your favourite chocolate
mints. Somebody must have eaten them. I suspect
Charlie.

ANGELA: The boatman?

TERRY: My driver. Minibus Charlie. How could you forget
Charlie? And the boatman's name is Carlin.

ANGELA: Give me a drink, Terry, would you?

TERRY: Wine? Gin? Vodka?

ANGELA: Anything at all. Just a drop.

BERNA: (*Suddenly stands up and proclaims:*) All right! I'll tell
my story now!

TRISH: Good girl, Berna.

BERNA: I had a different psychiatrist in the clinic last week, a
very intense young Englishman called Walsingham. He
told me this story.

ANGELA: (*Accepting drink from* TERRY) Thanks.

TERRY: Anybody else?

FRANK: Quiet.

TRISH: Attention, please. (*To* BERNA) 'Once upon a time . . . '

BERNA: Not once upon a time, Trish. I can give you the exact
date: 1294. And in the year 1294, in the village of

44

Nazareth, in the land that is now called Israel, a very wonderful thing happened. There was in the village a small, white-washed house built of rough stone, just like these; and for over a thousand years the villagers looked on that house as their most wonderful possession; because that house had been the home of Mary and Joseph and their baby, Jesus.

And then in the year 1294, on the seventh day of March, an amazing thing happened. That small, white-washed house rose straight up into the air, right away up into the sky. It hung there for a few seconds as if it were a bird finding its bearings. Then it floated – flew – over the Mediterranean Sea, high up over the island of Crete, across the Aegean Sea, until it came to the coast of Italy. It crossed that coast and came to a stop directly above a small town called Loreto in the centre of Italy. Then it began to descend, slowly down and down and down, until it came to rest in the centre of the town. And there it sits to this day. And it is known as the Holy House of Loreto – a place of pilgrimage, revered and attested to by hundreds of thousands of pilgrims every year. The Holy House of Loreto.

(*Nobody knows how to respond. Pause.*)

TRISH: A flying house? . . . And it's there now? . . . Well, heavens above, isn't that a –

BERNA: And because it took off and flew across the sea and landed safely again, all over the world Our Lady of Loreto is known as the Patron Saint of Aviation.

(*Another brief pause.*)

FRANK: There you are . . .

TRISH: (*Breezily*) Good girl, Berna.

FRANK: Never knew that . . .

TRISH: Live and learn.

FRANK: Indeed . . . live and learn . . .

45

TERRY: Wonderful story, Berna. Well done.

FRANK: Terry says this is my colour. What do you think?

BERNA: In our second year we had a lecturer in Equity, a Scotsman called – I've forgotten his name. We called him Offence to Reason because he used that phrase in every single lecture. We used to wait for it to come. 'Does that constitute an offence to reason?' (*Laughs.*) He was in awe of reason. He really believed reason was the key to 'truth', the 'big verities'.

TERRY: The sun's trying to come up, is it?

BERNA: No, it's not a wonderful story, Trish. It's a stupid story. And crude. And pig-headed. A flying house is an offence to reason, isn't it? It marches up to reason and belts it across the gob and says to it, 'Fuck you, reason. I'm as good as you any day. You haven't all the fucking answers – not by any means.' That's what Dr Walsingham's story says. And that's why I like it.
(*She begins to cry quietly.* TERRY *moves towards her. But* TRISH *holds up her hand and he stops. Then* TRISH *goes to* BERNA *and holds her.*)

TRISH: Shhh, love, shhh . . .

BERNA: (*Into* TRISH's *face*) It's defiance, Trish – that's what I like about it.

TRISH: I know . . . I know . . .

BERNA: It's stupid, futile defiance.

TRISH: Shh . . .
(*She moves away from* TRISH *and goes to the end of the pier. Her narrative has charged the atmosphere with unease, with anxiety.*)

FRANK: (*Breezily*) You're right, Terry; the sun is trying to come up.

TERRY: Yes?

FRANK: (*Sings*) 'Dear one, the world . . .' You and I could do a neat dance to that, Berna. Anybody know it?

46

TERRY: (*Sings*) '. . . is waiting for the sunrise – '
    (FRANK *and* TERRY *sing together*.)
TERRY and FRANK: 'Every rose is heavy with dew . . . '
FRANK: George?
TRISH: George is tired. He (FRANK) knows the words of
    everything. What sort of a head have you got?
FRANK: (*Brightly*) Full of rubbish. And panic. (*Sings*:) 'The
    thrush on high his sleepy mate is calling . . .' (*He fades
    out*.)
ANGELA: Did you bring a swimsuit, Berna?
    (*No answer*. BERNA *now moves up to the catwalk*.)
TRISH: (*To* BERNA) I brought mine. You can have mine.
FRANK: Or better still, Berna – I say, I say, I say – you may
    have mine!
ANGELA: We're all too tired, Frank.
FRANK: Are we? He sings the first two lines of the refrain of
    'Lazy River'. (*Brief pause*.) Right, Trish – all set?
TRISH: What?
FRANK: You're next!
TRISH: What's he talking about?
FRANK: For a story!
TERRY: Yes, Trish!
TRISH: I don't know any –
TERRY: You're a wonderful story-teller. Isn't she, Berna?
TRISH: Ah, come on, Terry. You know very well –
ANGELA: Go on, Trish!
FRANK: Any kind of fiction will do us.
ANGELA: Myth – fantasy –
TERRY: A funny story –
ANGELA: A good lie –
FRANK: Even a bad lie. Look at us for God's sake – we'll accept
    anything! Right, Berna?
    (*Now* TRISH *understands that their purpose is to engage*
    BERNA *again*.)

47

TRISH: You want a story? Right! (*She jumps to her feet and launches into her performance with great theatricality and brio.*) So I'm on then? All right--all right--all right!

FRANK: Certainly are.

TRISH: (*Stalling, improvising*) You want a story?

ANGELA: We need a story.

TERRY: Come down and hear this, Berna.

(BERNA *looks over the wall.*)

TRISH: A story. Absolutely. Yes. Once upon a time and a very long time ago –

TERRY: She's bluffing.

ANGELA: Terry!

TERRY: Look at her eyes.

FRANK: What do her eyes say, George?

ANGELA: (*To* TRISH) Pay no attention to him (TERRY). Once upon a time . . . ?

TRISH: May I proceed?

FRANK: Let the lady speak.

TERRY: That's no lady – that's-a ma sista.

ANGELA: Terry!

TRISH: Once upon a time and a very long time ago –

(FRANK *sings the first line of 'Just a Song at Twilight'.*)

ANGELA: Please, Frank.

(*Suddenly* TRISH *knows what her story is.*)

TRISH: The morning we got married, George! OK?

GEORGE: OK.

FRANK: Good one. Yeah.

ANGELA: What story's that?

TRISH: May I, George?

GEORGE: Go ahead.

ANGELA: I've forgotten that story.

TERRY: That's a boring story, Trish.

FRANK: Is it? Great! Boring is soothing.

ANGELA: Do I know the story?

48

FRANK: Boring reassures.

TERRY: 'Course you do.

FRANK: I'm all for boring. Sedate us, Trish.

TRISH: If I may continue . . . ?

FRANK: And it came to pass –

TRISH: Twenty-two years ago. Saint Theresa's Church.

FRANK: Parish of Drumragh.

TRISH: Ten o'clock Mass.

TERRY: Best man. (*Bows.*)

TRISH: And little Patricia, all a quiver in gold tiara, cream
chiffon dress and pale-blue shoes with three-quarter heels,
has left her home for the last time and –

FRANK: (*Sings*) 'There was I –' George?
(GEORGE *picks up his accordion.*)

TERRY: You were bridesmaid, Berna. Remember?

ANGELA: (*Remembering*) It's the story of the missing – !

FRANK: Don't! (*i.e., interrupt*)

TRISH: May I? She arrives at the door of Saint Theresa's. And
now her little heart starts to flutter because just as she
enters the church on her Daddy's arm, Miss Quirk begins
to play the harmonium –
(*She is suddenly drowned out by* GEORGE *playing the first line
of 'There was I' – which is immediately picked up by*
FRANK.)

FRANK: (*Sings*) '. . . waiting at the church –' That's it!
'Waiting at the church –' Terry!
(TERRY *and* FRANK *do a dance/march routine and sing
together:*)

FRANK and TERRY: 'Waiting at the church
When I found –'

FRANK: What?

TERRY: '– he'd left me in the lurch –' Angela!

ANGELA: (*Sings*) 'Oh, how it did upset me –'

TERRY and FRANK: (*Sing:*) 'Tra–la–la–la–la.'

49

ANGELA: Sorry, Trish.

TRISH: (*Pretended anger*) Fine – fine –

ANGELA: Behave yourselves, you two!

TRISH: Have your own fun.

FRANK: Please, Trish –

TRISH: No point, is there?

FRANK: Go on, Patricia: 'The flutter bride was all a-chiffon – '

TRISH: See?

TERRY: Anyhow we all know how the story ends, don't we?

FRANK: So what? All we want of a story is to hear it again and
again and again and again and again.

ANGELA: Are you going to let the girl finish?

FRANK: And so it came to pass . . .

(GEORGE *now plays Wagner's 'Wedding March' very softly,
with a reverence close to mockery.*)

TRISH: Thank you, George. (*She blows him a kiss.*) The church
is full to overflowing. My modest eyes are still on the
ground. Daddy's gaze is manfully direct. We walk up that
aisle together with quiet dignity until we come to the
altar –

FRANK: She's a natural!

TRISH: And then for the first time I raise those modest eyes so
that I can feast them on my handsome groom-to-be, my
beloved George.

FRANK: Yes?

TRISH: But lo –

FRANK: Go on!

TRISH: Who steps out to receive me – ?

FRANK: But –

TERRY: The anxious bookie – the groomsman!

FRANK: Groomsman? Where's the groom?

TRISH: No groom. No George.

(*Howls of dismay.*)

ANGELA: Shame, George, shame!

50

FRANK: Where can he be?

TERRY: (*Calls*) George!

FRANK: (*Calls*) We need you, George!

TERRY: (*Calls*) Where are you, George?

FRANK: (*Calls*) Heeelp!

FRANK and TERRY: (*Calls*) Heeelp!

ANGELA: Will you let the girl finish her story?

TRISH: Haven't seen him for over a week. Last heard from him two days ago from Limerick –

TERRY: Cork.

TRISH: – where the Aeolians – Michael Robinson and himself – they've been giving Beethoven recitals in schools and colleges there.

TERRY: Knew she'd get it wrong.

FRANK: (*To* TERRY) Please.

TRISH: But these concerts, I know, are finished. Why isn't he here?

TERRY: Playing with the Dude Ranchers.

TRISH: Why isn't he here for his wedding?

TERRY: Finishing a tour in County Cork.

TRISH: Terry, the Aeolians were in Limerick doing a series of –

TERRY: The Aeolians had broken up three months before you got married.

TRISH: Don't you think I might – ?

TERRY: George was working full-time with the Ranchers when you and he got married.

TRISH: Terry –

FRANK: Those details don't –

TERRY: That's why George packed in the Aeolians – to make some money – so that you and he could get married. Right, George?

ANGELA: So what? The point of Trish's story is –

TERRY: (*To* TRISH) You asked me to take George on. Don't you remember?

51

TRISH: So that when we – ?

TERRY: And that's when the Ranchers really took off. When he packed in the Aeolians and joined the Ranchers. He made the Ranchers. We would never have come to anything without George.

(TRISH *is totally bewildered.*)

TRISH: But how could I? . . . God . . . And when did – ?

TERRY: You've forgotten – that's all. (*He hugs her quickly.*) I'd signed George up three months before your wedding.

ANGELA: And all this has nothing to do with the story. The point is that he did turn up at Saint Theresa's – and only ten minutes late. Well done, George.

TERRY: (*To* TRISH) I didn't mean to –

TRISH: But how could I have – ?

FRANK: Certainly did turn up. On a motorbike – right? Soaked through and purple with cold.

ANGELA: With the wedding-suit in a rucksack on his back.

FRANK: Changed in the organ-loft – remember?

TRISH: Oh my God, how could that have happened?

ANGELA: That was a good day.

FRANK: Great day.

TERRY: (*To* TRISH) Sorry.

FRANK: A wonderful day . . . God . . . what a day that was . . .

ANGELA: Well done, Trish. A great story. The best story yet. Very well done.

(*Silence. Again they withdraw into themselves.* BERNA *now climbs from the catwalk up to the top wall. As she does she sings, without words, 'O, Mother, I could weep'. She walks along the top of the wall.* TERRY *now sees her.*)

TERRY: Berna, please come down from there.

FRANK: Berna.

TERRY: That is dangerous, Berna.

TRISH: (*To* TERRY) For God's sake bring her down!

ANGELA: Berna, love –

52

TERRY: (*Command*) Come down, Berna! At once!
 (BERNA, *still singing, is now at the end of the wall. Without looking at anybody she jumps into the sea.*)
FRANK: Berna!
TERRY: Jesus!
ANGELA: Berna!
TERRY: Oh Jesus Christ . . . !

ACT TWO

Before the lights go up we hear GEORGE *playing:*
> '*All things bright and beautiful, all creatures great and small*
> *All things wise and wonderful, the Good Lord made them all.*'

At that point lights up.

A new day has opened. A high sky. A pristine and brilliant morning sunlight that enfolds the pier like an aureole and renovates everything it touches.

BERNA, *a cardigan round her shoulders, is in different clothes – her Act One clothes are drying across a bollard.* TRISH *is brushing and combing* BERNA'*s hair.* TERRY *is up on the catwalk, looking casually across the landscape, occasionally using binoculars.* ANGELA *is playing a game she has invented. From a distance of about five feet she pitches stones (lobster-pot weights) at an empty bottle placed close to the lifebelt stand. (When the game ends there is a small mound of stones.) On the lifebelt stand now hangs – as well as Angela's sun hat from Act One – the silk scarf* BERNA *wore in Act One.* GEORGE *continues playing:*
> '*Each little flower that opens, each little bird that sings,*
> *He made their glowing colours, he made their tiny wings.*
> *All things bright and beautiful, all creatures great and*
> *small –*'

Now ANGELA *sings to the music:*

ANGELA: (*Sings*) 'All things wise and wonderful, the Good
    Lord made them all.' You are 'wise and wonderful',
    George: you're the only one of us that slept all night.
GEORGE: Did I?
ANGELA: For an hour. And you snore.

54

GEORGE: Sorry. (*He beckons her to him.*) If I ever decide to go, I want your children to have this (*accordion*).

ANGELA: You are going –

GEORGE: One of them might take it up.

ANGELA: George, that's –

GEORGE: Bit battered but it's working all right.

ANGELA: That's a lovely thought. (*She kisses him.*) Thank you.

GEORGE: *If* I ever decide to go.

TERRY: Where did Frank say he was going?

ANGELA: To take photographs, he said. Probably to beat the head off poor old Carlin.
(*Pause.*)

TERRY: Listen to those birds.

ANGELA: Larks, are they?

TERRY: 'And they heard the song of coloured birds.' You wouldn't believe me.

ANGELA: They're larks, Terry. Ordinary larks.
(GEORGE *begins to play 'Skylark' very softly.*)
Exactly, George.

TERRY: Has it a name, that game?

ANGELA: It's called: how close can you get without touching it? Anybody got the time?

TERRY: Just after seven.

BERNA: (*Looks at her watch*) Stopped. Salt water finished it.

ANGELA: When does the minibus come for us?

TERRY: Half an hour or so.
(BERNA *takes off her watch, shakes it and holds it to her ear.*)

BERNA: That's that.
(*She casually tosses it into the sea. Only* TRISH *sees this.*)

TERRY: There must be hundreds of them (*birds*). And they *are* coloured.

TRISH: (*Quietly*) You put the heart across us, Berna, jumping into the sea like that.

55

BERNA: Are you nearly finished? (*Hair-dressing.*)

TRISH: You shouldn't have done that.

BERNA: I wanted a swim.

TRISH: It was a naughty thing to do. It was a cruel thing to do.

BERNA: I told you – I wanted a swim.

TRISH: Particularly cruel to Terry.

BERNA: Oh, poor Terry. (*She stands up abruptly.*) That's fine, Trish. Thank you. (*To* ANGELA) May I play?

ANGELA: Of course.

TERRY: Well, would you look at that! Carlin has lit his fire again! (*Laughs.*) What a strange man.

ANGELA: (*To* BERNA) There are stones over there.

TERRY: Maybe he'll come for us after he's had his breakfast. What do you think?

TRISH: (*Wearily*) Terry.

ANGELA: (*To* TRISH) Going to play?

TRISH: Yes.

TERRY: We still have time for a quick dart out and straight back. We'd do it in less than an hour.

TRISH: D'you know what I would love? A cup of strong tea!

TERRY: There's still a chance. Why not? I'm offering five to one against. Three to one. Any takers?

(GEORGE *has come to the last line of 'Skylark'.* TRISH *sings the line.*)

TRISH: Now. Tell me what to do.

(*The music stops.*)

ANGELA: The aim is to get as close as possible to that bottle. But every time you touch it you lose a point.

TRISH: You *lose* a point? What sort of a makey-up game is that!

TERRY: Looks wonderful in this light (*the island*). I'm not giving up. Two to one against. Even money.

TRISH: We should all be exhausted, shouldn't we? But I feel . . . exhilarated. Play something exhilarating, George.

(*He plays 'Regina Caeli' right through.*)

56

(*Immediately he begins.*) That's not exhilarating, is it?

ANGELA: (*To* TRISH) Your throw.

BERNA: Is there a chill in the air?

TRISH: (*Preparing to throw*) Right.

(BERNA *reaches out to take her scarf from the lifebelt stand.*)

ANGELA: (*Quickly*) No; take mine. It's warmer. Like a hall stand, isn't it? Good one, Trish. You have the hang of it.

(BERNA *drapes Angela's scarf around her shoulders.* FRANK *enters.*)

FRANK: Well–well–well! What Eden is this? And what happy people have we here, besporting themselves in the sunlight?

TERRY: (*Coming down*) We thought we had lost you.

FRANK: For you, George. Found it in the sand dunes back there.

(*Music stops.*)

GEORGE: Yes?

FRANK: Interesting, isn't it? Polished flint-stone. The head of an axe, I think.

GEORGE: Thank you.

FRANK: That's the hole for the handle. Beautifully shaped, isn't it?

GEORGE: Lovely.

TERRY: Where did you find it?

FRANK: Just behind the pier. Probably buried in the sand at one time. Then the sand shifted.

TERRY: May I see it?

GEORGE: Thank you, Frank.

FRANK: Some weapon. That's a lethal edge there.

TERRY: And the weight of it.

FRANK: We'll make a handle for it; and on your next tour, if audiences aren't appreciative enough – (*He mimes striking with the axe.*)

TERRY: That *is* sharp.

57

FRANK: Meant for business, that weapon.

TERRY: Did you get some good pictures?

FRANK: Don't talk to me about pictures! Tell you all in a moment. (*He goes to* BERNA *and presents her with a bunch of wild flowers.*) For you, my lady. (*He kisses her.*)

BERNA: Oh, Frank.

ANGELA: Aren't they pretty? Look at that blue.

TRISH: You got them around here?

FRANK: Just over the sand dunes.

TRISH: (*To* GEORGE) He's a *real* gentleman.

FRANK: (*To* BERNA) And d'you know what? – I could eat you in that dress.

BERNA: They're beautiful, Frank. Thank you.

FRANK: Welcome.

ANGELA: Now – Berna (*the game*).

TRISH: You want to know how it's really done, girls? Just watch this.

(*They continue playing.*)

TERRY: Lovely flowers. Thank you.

FRANK: The place is full of them.

TERRY: We thought maybe you'd gone to chastise Mr Carlin.

FRANK: Just before daybreak there was a white mist suspended above the island; like a white silk canopy. And as the sun got up you could see the mist dissolve and vanish. So of course I thought: Oilean Draoichta emerging from behind its veil – capture this for posterity!

TERRY: Did you get it?

FRANK: Two bloody spools of it. Wasted all my film.

ANGELA: (*To* TRISH) Not bad. Not bad.

TRISH: Not bad? Wonderful!

BERNA: Very close, Trish. Good one.

TRISH: I think this could well be my game. Want to play, Frank?

Listen to this. You won't believe what I saw
rish.

.)
d you see, Frank?

ks at them. He is not sure if he will tell his story.)
_____ the last wisp of the veil was melting away,
suddenly – as if it had been waiting for a sign – suddenly a
dolphin rose up out of the sea. And for thirty seconds,
maybe a minute, it danced for me. Like a faun, a satyr;
with its manic, leering face. Danced with a deliberate,
controlled, exquisite abandon. Leaping, twisting,
tumbling, gyrating in wild and intricate contortions. And
for that thirty seconds, maybe a minute, I could swear it
never once touched the water – was free of it – had
nothing to do with water. A performance – that's what it
was. A performance so considered, so aware, that you
knew it knew it was being witnessed, wanted to be
witnessed. Thrilling; and wonderful; and at the same time
– I don't know why – at the same time . . . with that
manic, leering face . . . somehow very disturbing.
BERNA: Did you get pictures of it?
FRANK: Nothing. You'd almost think it waited until my last
shot was used up before it appeared. Thirty seconds,
maybe a minute . . . Unbelievable. (*Embarrassed laugh.*)
Another apparition, Terry.
TERRY: Maybe.
(*Pause.* FRANK *is now embarrassed at his own intensity and
because the others are all staring at him. He laughs again.*)
FRANK: So I saw a porpoise or a dolphin or something leap out
of the water and dance about a bit. Wonderful!
TRISH: I love dolphins. I think they are terrific. (*Briskly*)
Right. Who's next?
(ANGELA, TRISH *and* BERNA *play their game.*)

59

FRANK: Left them speechless, didn't it? – my Ballybeg
    epiphany.
TERRY: Sorry I missed that.
FRANK: (*To* GEORGE) Upset me, that damn thing, for some
    reason.
    (BERNA *nods and smiles.*)
TERRY: Drink?
FRANK: (*Gestures no.*) Could have done with one back there. It
    really was a ceremonial dance, Terry – honest to God.
    And they look so damned knowing – don't they? – with
    those almost human faces . . . I'm getting to like this
    (*jacket*).
TERRY: Well, what are our chances?
FRANK: Chances?
    (TERRY *indicates Carlin's house.*)
    Forget him. Next time we'll bring our own boat.
TERRY: Sorry. Not allowed.
FRANK: Maybe you're right. Maybe he still will come. Who's
    to say?
    (TERRY *moves to the end of the pier where he sits by himself.*)
ANGELA: That hit the bottle. Point lost, Trish.
TRISH: Didn't hit it, did it?
ANGELA: Sorry. Point down. Berna?
    (BERNA, *her flowers still in her hand, picks up a stone close to*
    FRANK. *At the same time she puts one of her flowers in her*
    hair and blows a kiss to him. As she does this GEORGE *plays*
    'Bring Flowers of the Rarest:
      '*Bring flowers of the rarest, bring blossoms the fairest*
      From garden and woodland and hillside and dale
      Our full hearts are swelling, our glad voices telling
      The praise of the loveliest flower of the vale.'
TRISH: (*Immediately after* GEORGE *plays the first line and as he*
    continues playing) I know that song, don't I?
FRANK: So do I.

BERNA: It's a hymn – is it?

GEORGE: Guess.

FRANK: It *is* a hymn – isn't it?

BERNA: Play the chorus, George.

TRISH: I do know it, whatever it is.

FRANK: I do, too.

(GEORGE *now begins the chorus: 'O Mary, we crown thee with blossoms today –'*)

TRISH: Yes! (*Sings*) ' – Queen of the angels and queen of the May –'

FRANK: Haven't heard that since I was a child.

TRISH and BERNA: (*Sing*) 'O Mary, we crown thee with blossoms today, Queen of the angels and queen of the May.'

(*To* GEORGE) Thank you.

FRANK: Not since I was a child.

(*Brief pause. And immediately* ANGELA *plunges into 'O Dem Golden Slippers'. And as she sings,* GEORGE *accompanies her. She picks up Frank's shoes, and singing loudly, raucously, defiantly, and waving the shoes above her head she parades/ dances around the pier. She sings the entire chorus. She stops suddenly. The performance is over. Pause. Now she sings very softly the first two lines of the chorus of 'I Don't Know Why I'm Happy'. She tails off listlessly. She looks at the shoes and tosses them over to where* FRANK *is sitting. She looks at them all.*)

ANGELA: What a goddamn, useless, endless, unhappy outing this has been! (*Pause.*) I'm sorry, Terry . . .
(*Pause.*)

FRANK: (*To* TERRY) May I (*drink*)? (*He pours a drink and scoops up water.*) Should do a rain dance. Well's almost dry.
(TERRY *now rises and joins them.*)

TERRY: I just remembered – I do have a story.

TRISH: Too late, Terry. Story time's over.

FRANK: No, it's not. It's always story time. Right, Berna?

61

BERNA: Is it?

FRANK: Certainly is.

TRISH: All right. But make it short, Terry. Short and funny. I need a laugh.

FRANK: Terence . . . ?

TERRY: Yes. Well. The solicitor who is handling the sale of Oilean Draoichta – he told me this story. We were having lunch together. No; we had finished eating. He was having coffee and I was having tea and we both –

TRISH: The story, Terry.

TERRY: (*Almost reluctantly*) Yes – yes – the story. Well, the story he told me was this. Many years ago a young man was killed out there.

BERNA: Killed how?

TERRY: I suppose . . . murdered.

FRANK: God.

TERRY: His name was Sean O'Boyle. He was seventeen years of age. If you were to believe my solicitor friend he was . . . ritually killed.

TRISH: What do you mean?

TERRY: A group of young people – he was one of them – seven young men and seven young women. It wasn't a disagreement, a fight; nothing like that. They were all close friends.

ANGELA: And what happened?

TERRY: The evidence suggests some sort of ritual, during which young O'Boyle was . . . (*He shrugs.*)

TRISH: Oh, my God.

BERNA: What evidence?

TERRY: Burned-out fires – empty wine bottles – clothes left behind – blood smeared on rocks. It's thought there was some sort of orgy. Anyhow, at some point they dismembered him. That's accurate enough – from the pieces they found.

62

FRANK: Jesus Christ, Terry . . . oh, Jesus Christ . . .

ANGELA: When did this happen?

TERRY: 1932. On the night of June 26.

ANGELA: These young people – they were from here?

TERRY: Part of a group from this parish who had just returned
from Dublin from the Eucharistic Congress. The older
people went straight to their homes. The young group –
our fourteen – apparently they had been drinking all the
way home from Dublin – they stole a half-decker – from
this pier actually – and headed out for Oilean Draoichta.
Some people say they had poitin stashed out there and
that one of the girls was a great fiddler and that they just *Dionysus*
went out to have a dance. My friend has his own theory.
These people were peasants, from a very remote part of
the country. And he believes they were still in a state of
intoxication after the Congress – it was the most
spectacular, the most incredible thing they had ever
witnessed. And that ferment and the wine and the music
and the dancing . . .

TRISH: I don't know what you're saying, Terry.

TERRY: That young O'Boyle was . . . sacrificed.

FRANK: Jesus Christ.

BERNA: The other thirteen – they were charged?

TERRY: No charges were ever brought.

TRISH: Why not?

ANGELA: The police weren't brought in?

TERRY: Oh, yes. But by then the situation was away beyond
their control. The parish was in uproar. Passions were at
boiling point. Families were physically attacking one
another. The police were helpless. The only person who
could control the situation was the bishop of the time. He
had led the group that had just made the pilgrimage to the
Eucharistic Congress. And every year on August 15 he
organized a pilgrimage out to the island.

63

TRISH: So?

TERRY: So the thirteen were summoned to the bishop's palace. All that is known is that they made a solemn pledge never to divulge what happened that night on the island; that they had to leave the country immediately and for ever, and that before the end of the week they had all left for Australia.

TRISH: Oh, my God.

BERNA: So nobody was ever charged?

TERRY: Nobody. O'Boyle was an only child. Both his parents were dead within the year.

ANGELA: Oilean Draoichta – wonderful.

TERRY: Then the war came. Times were bad. People moved away. Within ten years the area was depopulated – that's your derelict church back there, Frank. The local belief was that the whole affair brought a curse on the parish and that nothing would ever prosper here again.

FRANK: Jesus Christ, what a story! Jesus Christ, we don't know half of what goes on in the world!

TERRY: (*To* TRISH) I'm sure that's the real reason why the pilgrimage out there really petered out. Couldn't have survived that.

TRISH: Damn you, Terry Martin, how could you have brought us out to a place like that?

TERRY: Trish, it is just an –

TRISH: And how could you have bought an evil place like that?

TERRY: The place is not evil, Trish.

TRISH: I hate that story. That's a hateful story. You shouldn't have told us that story.

(*She moves quickly away and busies herself with her belongings. Silence.*)

BERNA: (*To* FRANK) These grew (*her flowers*).

FRANK: What's that?

BERNA: He said nothing ever grew again. These did.

64

FRANK: True . . . that's true . . . Going to be another warm day.

TERRY: Think so?

FRANK: Yes. Very warm. Wonderful.

(*They all drift apart.*)

TRISH: Shouldn't we tidy the place up a bit? Carlin could arrive any time.

BERNA: You mean Charlie, don't you?

TRISH: Do I? Whatever.

(*They begin tidying up, each attending to his/her own belongings. First they put on their shoes. Then* TERRY *puts bottles, flasks, etc., back into the hampers.* TRISH *folds up sleeping-bags and packs her other belongings.* BERNA *folds her now dry clothes and puts them away.* FRANK *looks after his cameras, binoculars, etc.* ANGELA *makes a pile of the paper napkins, plastic cups, etc., scattered around the pier.* GEORGE *watches the others at their tasks. While all this tidying up is taking place, the following episodes happen:*

BERNA *takes her scarf off the lifebelt stand and puts it round her neck. Then she sees Angela's hat.*)

BERNA: Isn't this your hat, Angela?

ANGELA: Thanks.

BERNA: Do you want it?

ANGELA: My good hat for God's sake! Why wouldn't I want it? Thank you. The only sun hat I have.

(BERNA *hands the hat to* ANGELA. *A moment's hesitation. Then she removes the scarf from her neck and knots it on one of the arms of the stand.* FRANK *witnesses this episode.*)

TRISH: (*To* GEORGE) I'll take that (*accordion*).

GEORGE: Why?

TRISH: What d'you mean 'why'? I'll put it in the case for you.

GEORGE: Why?

TRISH: Because we're about to – Fine – fine! Suit yourself!

GEORGE: Yes.

(TRISH *moves away from him.* FRANK *goes to the stand, takes off his belt and buckles it round the upright. Now he sees* TERRY *watching him.*)

FRANK: (*Breezily*) Maybe that's a bit reckless, is it? D'you think they'll stay up by themselves?

TERRY: I'm all for a gamble.

FRANK: Pot belly. Safe enough.

(TRISH *witnesses this episode.* TRISH *looks at the mound of stones.*)

TRISH: Should we put these back where we found them?

BERNA: I wouldn't bother. They were scattered all over the place when we got here.

(TRISH *goes to the stand. She takes off her bracelet and hangs it on one of the arms, balancing* BERNA's *scarf. Then she goes back to* GEORGE, *who is standing immobile beside their belongings.*)

TRISH: Give me your handkerchief.

(GEORGE *does not move.* TRISH *takes the handkerchief out of his breast pocket, returns to the stand and knots the handkerchief beside her bracelet.*)

ANGELA: (*To* TERRY) Did you say you had honey cake?

TERRY: Yes. Are you hungry? (*He produces the cake from the hamper. A sealed tin.*) How do you open this thing?

ANGELA: No, no; don't open it. I'll leave it here, I think. (*She places the tin on top of a bollard.*)

TERRY: What are you doing?

ANGELA: For Carlin. You don't mind, do you? He's sure to come snooping around after we've gone. A present.

TERRY: Will you ever come back here?

ANGELA: Just to keep him sweet.

BERNA: Is this yours, Frank (*camera case*)?

FRANK: Just looking for that. Thank you.

ANGELA: (*To* TERRY) Sorry for that outburst a while ago.

TERRY: Please . . .

66

ANGELA: It was a lovely birthday.

TERRY: We'll not talk about that. Interesting place, though.

ANGELA: Pretty.

TERRY: Wonderful, isn't it?

ANGELA: (*Gesturing to the island*) I can live without all that stuff, Terry. Honestly. Housework – the kids – teaching – bills – Frank – doctors – more bills – just getting through every day is about as much as I can handle; more than I can handle at times. (*Remembering that the island is his*) I really wish you luck with it. Yes–yes–yes, of course it's wonderful – beautiful and wonderful.

TERRY: When will I see you?

ANGELA: Terry –

TERRY: Next Sunday?

ANGELA: No. Please.

(*She spreads her hands as if to say, 'What's the point? Can't you see there's no point?' Then, very quickly, she takes his hands in hers, squeezes them, and then swiftly moves away from him.* FRANK *has found a small bottle. He holds it up.*)

FRANK: Anybody mind if I pour this out? (*Reads*) Cherry Brandy. (*He empties it out.*) God, that's a sin, isn't it? (*Now he picks up a plastic cup, scoops whatever water is left in the 'well' and pours it into the brandy bottle. Now he is aware that* TERRY *and* ANGELA *are watching him. He laughs.*) For a quick shot on the way home. In case Charlie's jokes get too bad. Hardly any (*water*) left . . . (*He corks the bottle with paper tissues.* TRISH *goes to the small pile of rubbish (paper tissues, plastic cups, etc.) that* ANGELA *gathered. She strikes a match. Just as she is about to set fire to the refuse,* ANGELA *rushes to her and stamps the fire out with her foot.*)

ANGELA: For God's sake, woman!

TRISH: What have I – ?

ANGELA: You can't light a fire here! (*Calm again*) We can take this away with us, can't we? That would be simpler, wouldn't it?

(*And she begins piling the rubbish into a plastic bag.*)

TRISH: (*Excessive astonishment*) Oh good Lord, we're suddenly very house-proud, aren't we?

(ANGELA *puts her hand on* TRISH's *elbow.*)

ANGELA: Sorry, Trish. Could do with some sleep.

(*She moves away to the end of the pier and looks around. The various tasks have been completed.*)

FRANK: Now, Terry. Yourself.

TERRY: What's that?

FRANK: You're going to leave a visiting card, aren't you?

TERRY: A visiting – ?

FRANK: On the stand. 'Terry Martin Was Here.'

TERRY: (*Laughs*) Nothing to leave. (*Produces coins.*) Is money any good?

TRISH: Useless, Terry.

TERRY: What else can I give you?

FRANK: What else can he give us? What about that shirt?

(*Suddenly everybody is listening, watching.*)

BERNA: Yes, Terry. The shirt.

FRANK: Is the shirt what we want?

TRISH: The shirt will do.

BERNA: We want the shirt!

TRISH: Hand it over, Terry.

TERRY: Ah, come on now –

FRANK: We all want the shirt, don't we?

GEORGE: Yes–yes–yes!

(*Now* TRISH *sings rapidly – and keeps singing again and again:* 'I want the shirt – I want the shirt'; *to the air of* 'Here Comes the Bride'.)

FRANK: We'll take it now, Terry.

BERNA: We want it now, Terry, now.

TERRY: Here – I'll give you a pen-knife – matches –

FRANK: No good. The shirt, Terry. Hand it over.

(TERRY *tries to back away from them. They encircle him. They sing with* TRISH:)

ALL: 'We want the shirt – we want the shirt – (*etc.*)'

TERRY: My shoes! My shoes and socks –

BERNA: The shirt, Terry.

TRISH: The shirt – the shirt!

FRANK: The shirt – the shirt – the shirt!

(*All sing again,* 'We want the shirt – we want the shirt – '
GEORGE *starts playing 'Here comes the bride'.*)

TERRY: For God's sake, this is the only shirt I have here!

FRANK: Grab him!

TERRY: Frank – !

(*And suddenly they all grab him (all except* ANGELA *who is by herself at the end of the pier – but watching).* TERRY *falls to the ground. They pull at his shirt. As they do, overlapping:*)

BERNA: We have him!

FRANK: Hold his feet!

TERRY: For God's sake!

TRISH: Give it to us!

FRANK: Hold him – hold him!

TRISH: We want it – we want it!

TERRY: Help!

BERNA: Want it – want it – want it!

FRANK: Want it, Terry – want it!

BERNA: Pull – pull – pull!

TRISH: I've got it!

BERNA: Rip it off!

TERRY: Angela, help – !

FRANK: Hold his hands!

BERNA: Need it – need it!

TRISH: Got it! Yes!

TERRY: Please – !

FRANK: Pull – pull – pull!

(GEORGE *stops playing. Now* FRANK *stands up in triumph, a portion of Terry's shirt held aloft.*)

There!

TRISH: Well done, Frank.

BERNA: Now hang it up, Terry. (*To* ALL) Yes?

GEORGE: Yes – yes!

TRISH: Hang it up there, Terry. Come on – be a sport!

(TERRY *gets to his feet and pulls the remnant of his shirt together.*)

TERRY: Happy now, are you?

FRANK: On the lifebelt stand. Has to be done in person.

TERRY: You're a shower of bastards – you know that.

(*He takes the piece of the shirt and hangs it up. They applaud.*)

BERNA: Terry Martin Was Here.

TERRY: Satisfied?

TRISH: Wonderful!

TERRY: OK?

FRANK: You'll be remembered here for ever, Terry.

TERRY: Happy now? I hope you're all happy now.

BERNA: Don't be such a crank.

FRANK: Bit of fun, Terry. That's all.

TERRY: (*Relenting*) Not a button left.

FRANK: Just passing the time – killing time.

TERRY: And I could have split my head on those stones!

FRANK: Just a bit of fun.

(FRANK *goes to one of his bags and produces a shirt.*)

TRISH: You look wonderful, Terry. Doesn't he?

FRANK: This should fit you.

(TERRY *raises his hand in a pretended gesture of striking him.*)

And it's your colour.

TERRY: I like this now. I'm not going to part with it.

Bastards . . .

70

*(The moment has passed. They finish tidying up. They look
around the pier, now restored to what it was when they
arrived.)*

TRISH: So . . .

BERNA: So . . .

*(They look like people at a station – some standing – some
sitting – just waiting patiently to get away.)*

TRISH: Lovely harvest day, isn't it?

BERNA: What time is it now?

FRANK: Coming up to seven thirty.

*(Brief pause. FRANK sees two stones a few feet away from
the mound of stones. He picks one up and places it on top of
the mound.)*

Simple domestic instincts . . . *(He now picks up the second
stone and places it on top of the mound. (To TERRY) At
seven thirty in the morning the rage for the absolute isn't
quite so consuming . . . The acceptance of what is . . .
(Brief pause.)*

ANGELA: He's out there somewhere, just below the surface.

TERRY: Who's that?

ANGELA: His dancing porpoise.

FRANK: Damn right. Waiting for an audience.

TERRY: Not many audiences around here.

FRANK: Or maybe just searching for the other thirteen.
Who's to say?
(Short pause.)

TRISH: Is he punctual?

TERRY: *(Laughs)* Carlin?

TRISH: *(Wearily)* God! Your driver – Charlie!

TERRY: He'll be on time. He's always on bloody time.
(Short pause.)

TRISH: *(To GEORGE)* Are you not going to put that into the
case?

GEORGE: No.

TRISH: What's got into you?

GEORGE: I'm not finished playing.

(*Short pause.* ANGELA *is still by herself at the end of the pier.*)

ANGELA: There was a city called Eleusis in Attica in ancient
Greece; and every year at the end of summer, religious
ceremonies were held there in honour of Demeter, the
goddess of the harvest – what we would call a harvest
festival. And they were known as the Eleusinian Mysteries.

FRANK: Off again!

TRISH: No more stories, Angela. Let's get back to real life.

ANGELA: All we know about the ceremonies is that they began
with a period of fasting; that there was a ritual purification
in the sea; and that young people went through a ceremony
of initiation. And there was music and dancing and
drinking. And we know, too, that sacrifice was offered.
And that's about all we know. Because the people who took
part in the ceremonies vowed never to speak of what
happened there. So that when the civilization came to an
end it took the secrets of the Eleusinian Mysteries with it.

FRANK: What's your point – that they had bishops too? I'll tell
you something: it's going to be another roaster of a day.

(*Brief pause.*)

BERNA: Play something for us, George.

GEORGE: What?

BERNA: Whatever gives you pleasure.

GEORGE: My pleasure . . . right . . .

(*He strikes a few chords as he wonders what he will play. Then
suddenly:*)

TRISH: Shh! Listen! Listen!

BERNA: What is it?

TRISH: Stop! Quiet! Stop!

FRANK: Is it – ?

TRISH: The minibus! Isn't it? Listen!

FRANK: I don't hear –

72

BERNA: It is! She's right!

TRISH: At last! At last!

TERRY: Told you he was bloody punctual.

(*They are all suddenly animated, excited, joyous. They pick up their belongings. They all talk at the same time.*)

FRANK: Good old Charlie!

TERRY: Whose is this?

TRISH: What new jokes will he have?

ANGELA: Don't forget your sleeping-bag.

BERNA: We'll be home by lunchtime.

ANGELA: Can you manage all that?

FRANK: You're sun-burned.

GEORGE: Am I?

FRANK: Your forehead.

TRISH: The moment I get home – straight to bed!

FRANK: You're very lucky to have Charlie.

(*And gradually as the minibus gets closer, their chatter and their excitement die away. Now the minibus has arrived. The engine is switched off. FRANK goes to the exit.*)

Good man, Charlie. With you in a moment. (*He now sees the tin of honey cake and picks it up.*) What's this?

TERRY: That's for Carlin.

FRANK: Like hell. I'm taking –

TERRY: Leave it, Frank.

FRANK: Sorry . . .

(*Nobody moves, they look around. Nobody speaks. Finally:*)

TRISH: Nice place all the same . . . Isn't it?

FRANK: Lovely.

TRISH: It really is, Terry.

BERNA: So peaceful.

TRISH: Lovely.

FRANK: Really peaceful.

TRISH: Wonderful.

FRANK: Wonderful.

73

TRISH: (*To* GEORGE) Isn't it wonderful?

GEORGE: Yes.

TERRY: Angela's right: it was a mess, the whole thing.

FRANK: Terry –

TERRY: The least said . . . I just feel I've let you all down.

FRANK: Don't say another word. It was a great birthday party.
We had a wonderful time.

TRISH: He's right, Terry. Terrific.

FRANK: Thank you. And we'll do it again some time. (*To* ALL)
Agreed? (*To* GEORGE) Right, George?
(GEORGE *spreads his hands and smiles*.)
Only this time I'll take Mr Carlin in hand and he'll do
what he's supposed to do.

TRISH: And even though we don't make it out there –

FRANK: Of course we'll make it! Why wouldn't we make it?

TRISH: Well, at least now we know . . . it's there.

FRANK: (*Calls*) 'Bye, Conall!

TRISH: (*Calls*) 'Bye, Conall!
(FRANK *sings 'Aloha'*.)

TERRY: I should tell you –

TRISH: (*Calls*) Be good, Conall!

TERRY: I should have said –

FRANK: Trish, my love, you're looking nowhere near it.

TRISH: What do you – ?
(FRANK *turns her head to the right*.)

FRANK: Got it now?

TRISH: Ah.

FRANK: Still County Sligo.

TRISH: I know it's County Sligo, Frank.

FRANK: (*To* ALL) See? Nothing changes.

ANGELA: (*To* TERRY) You should have told us what?

TERRY: Nothing.

ANGELA: What should you have told us?

TERRY: (*Reluctantly*) What I said yesterday afternoon – this

74

morning – I'm confused – when was it? – anyhow, when I told you I owned the island, that *is* true – well, partially true. I *have* taken an option on it. The option expires in a month. And I'm not going to pick it up.

TRISH: Now that's the best news I've heard all day! The moment you told that story about –

(TERRY *holds up his hand to silence her.*)

TERRY: I want to pick it up. Oh, yes. Trouble is – I haven't the money. The bookie business – concert promotion – the last few years have been disastrous. And I'm afraid – (*Laughs*) – not to put a tooth in it – I'm broke.

TRISH: But, Terry, you –

TERRY: Things will pick up. The tide will turn. I'll rise again. Oh, yes, I'll rise again. (*To* BERNA) That's why I didn't tell you I'd optioned it. Knew I'd lose it. (*To* ALL) Actually I didn't mean to tell anybody . . . Look at those solemn faces! (*Laughs.*)To own Oilean Draoichta for two whole months – wasn't that wonderful enough? Wasn't that a terrific secret to have? Anyway . . . One small thing. I'd be glad if you kept it to yourselves – that I'm broke. Don't want a hundred creditors descending on me.

BERNA: I'm sorry, Terry.

TERRY: So we'll come back again, will we? What d'you say?

TRISH: But, Terry, how can you – ?

TERRY: When will we come back?

FRANK: Good God, Terry, how can you – ?

TERRY: Next year? What about next year?

FRANK: If I'd known – if any of us had any idea you were –

TERRY: My birthday next year – right?

FRANK: And you've been doling out – day after day – month after –

ANGELA: (*Triumphantly*) Yes, we will! Next year – and the year after – and the year after that! Because we want to! Not

out of need – out of desire! Not in expectation – but to
attest, to affirm, to acknowledge – to shout Yes, Yes, Yes!
Damn right we will, Terry! Yes – yes – yes!

FRANK: Twelve months' time – agreed?

TRISH: Agreed!

FRANK: Berna?

BERNA: Yes!

FRANK: George?

GEORGE: Agreed!

FRANK: No more talk! Settled! (*Calls*) 'Bye, Conall! 'Bye, lads.
They're waving to us! Wave back to them!

(FRANK *waves vigorously*. TRISH, GEORGE *and* BERNA
make smaller gestures.)

TRISH: 'Bye!

FRANK: (*Calls*) Terry's birthday next year! And for a whole
night!

(*They all join in, overlapping*:)

TRISH: 'Bye, sheep!

GEORGE: 'Bye.

TRISH: 'Bye, cattle.

TERRY: 'Bye, coloured birds.

BERNA: 'Bye, whin bush.

FRANK: 'Bye, bell.

TERRY: 'Bye, clothes on bushes.

ANGELA: 'Bye, low hill.

GEORGE: 'Bye.

TRISH: 'Bye, oak trees.

ANGELA: 'Bye, apple trees.

TERRY: 'Bye, Conall.

ALL: 'Bye . . . 'bye . . . 'bye . . .

FRANK: 'Bye, dancing dolphin . . . 'bye . . .

(*Still nobody moves. Now* GEORGE *plays in his 'sacred' style*:
'*Come, my love, come, my boat lies low
She lies high and dry on the O–hi–o*

76

*Come, my love, come, and come along with me
And I'll take you back to Tennessee.'*)

TRISH: Charlie's waiting for us. Shouldn't we make a move?
(*But nobody does. Now* BERNA *begins to hum with the song,
beginning with the first verse:*)

BERNA: (*Hums*) 'Down by the cane-brake close by the mill
     There lived a blue-eyed girl and her name was Nancy
     Dill . . . '

(GEORGE *accompanies her. Now* TERRY *hums with her:*)

TERRY *and* BERNA: (*Hum*) 'I told her that I loved her, I loved
her very long
     I'm going to serenade her and this will be my
song . . . '

(*Now* TRISH *and* FRANK *join in the humming:*)

TERRY, BERNA, TRISH *and* FRANK: 'Come, my love, come, my
     boat lies low
     She lies high and dry on the O-hi-o
     Come my love, come, come along with me
     And I'll take you back to Tennessee . . . '

(*They play / hum another verse and this time* ANGELA *joins
them. And this continues to the end of the play.*)

TRISH *goes to the mound of stones. She walks around it once.
Then she picks up a stone from the bottom of the mound and
places it on the top. Then she walks around the mound a
second time and again she places a stone on top. Then she goes
to the lifebelt stand and lightly touches her votive offering.
Then she goes to her belongings, picks them up and slowly
moves off.*

The moment TRISH *completes her first encircling* BERNA *joins
her. First she places the flowers* FRANK *gave her at the foot of
the stand. Then she does the ritual that* TRISH *is doing.
And this ceremony – encircling, lifting a stone, encircling,
lifting a stone, touching the votive offering – is repeated by
every character.* FRANK *immediately behind* BERNA, TERRY

77

immediately after FRANK. *And when they finish they pick up*
their belongings and – still humming to GEORGE's
accompaniment – move slowly off. Now only GEORGE *and*
ANGELA *are left.* GEORGE *stops playing. He looks at her and*
gestures towards the mound.)

ANGELA: You go ahead, George, I think I'll pass.
(*She watches him as he does the ritual. When he has finished*
he stands beside her, puts his arm on hers. They take a last
look round.)

GEORGE: Nice place.

ANGELA: Nice place.
(*She nods in agreement.*)

GEORGE: You'll come back some day.

ANGELA: I don't think –

GEORGE: Yes, you will. Some day. And when you do, do it for
me. No, no, I don't mean *for* me – just in memory of me.
(*She looks at him for a second. Then quickly, impetuously, she*
catches his head between her hands and kisses him. Then she
breaks away from him, rushes to the stand, kisses her sun hat
and hangs it resolutely on the very top of the stand.)

ANGELA: (*Defiantly*) For you, George! For both of us!
(*She rushes back to him, takes his arm and begins singing*
'Down By the cane-brake' loudly, joyously, happily – and he
accompanies her with comparable brio. The others (off) join
in.

GEORGE *and* ANGELA *exit. The engine starts up. The singing*
and the engine compete. Both sounds are encompassed by the
silence and complete stillness and gradually surrender to it.)

Do this in memory of me...

78

ACKNOWLEDGEMENTS

'The World is Waiting for the Sunrise' Copyright © 1919, Chappell Music Ltd., London. Reproduced by permission of International Music Publications Ltd.

'I Want to be Happy' Copyright © 1920, Harms Inc., USA, Warner Chappell Music Ltd., London. Reproduced by permission of International Music Publications Ltd.

'Jolly Good Company' Copyright © 1931, Campbell, Connelly & Co. Ltd., 8–9 Frith Street, London WIV 5TZ. Used by permission, all rights reserved.

'There I Was Waiting at the Church' Copyright © 1906. Reproduced by permission of Francis Day and Hunter Ltd., London WC2H OEA.

'Down in de Cane-brake' Copyright © 1928, Forster Music Pub Inc., USA. Reproduced by permission of Francis Day and Hunter Ltd., London WC2H OEA

'Heavenly Sunshine' Copyright © 1970, Al Gallico Music Corp., USA. Reproduced by permission of EMI Music Publishing Ltd., London WC2H OEA

Every effort has been made to contact all copyright holders of songs quoted in the text of this play. In case of any queries, please contact Curtis Brown Group Ltd., 162–168 Regent Street, London WIR 5TB.

music: Happy Days Are Here Again
el Want to be Happy
Jesu, Joy of Man's Desiring
Aloha
the the Good Old Summertime. Amas.
el Don't Know Why el'm Happy.
Here we are Again, Happy as can be.
Happy Birthday to You

Falling in Love Again
Heavenly Sunshine
Knees Up, Mother Brown
Abide with Me
O Mothers, el could mump for mirth.

Oh in the Stilly Night
Down by the Cane Brake
Regina Caeli
Beethoven's Sonata #14
Dear Oh, the World is Waiting
     for the Sunrise.

Happy River
Just a Song at Twilight
Then was el Waiting at the Church
Wagner's Wedding March.

All Things Bright & Beautiful
Skylark
Bring Flowers of the Rarest